Holy Women of the Past
and what they have to teach us today

Holy Women of the Past
and what they have to teach us today

Barbara B. Gardner

CALVARY PRESS PUBLISHING
CALVARYPRESS.COM

© 2009, Barbara B. Gardner

ALL RIGHTS RESERVED

Duplication by any means, photomechanical, electronic, or otherwise is strictly prohibited apart from prior written permission from the publisher.

Calvary Press Publishing
www.calvarypress.com

ISBN-13: 978-1-879737-65-5
ISBN-10: 1-879737-65-5

1. Christianity—Women's Issues
2. Practical Christianity
3. Bible Study

PRINTED IN THE UNITED STATES OF AMERICA

Contents

Eve—Mother of Life ❧ *9*

Mary—Blessed Among Women ❧ *31*

Sarah—Cherished Princess ❧ *59*

Naomi and Ruth—An Oasis of Faithfulness ❧ *101*

Deborah—A Woman of Victory ❧ *119*

The Shunammite Woman—Compelled by God ❧ *135*

Martha and Mary—Women Learning from Jesus ❧ *145*

Proverbs 31—An Excellent Wife ❧ *169*

Hannah—A Visionary Mother ❧ *187*

Abigail—Perceptive and Beautiful Messenger ❧ *201*

Priscilla—A Woman's Drive for Ministry ❧ *215*

Rahab the Prostitute—Saved Alive by God ❧ *237*

1

EVE — MOTHER OF LIFE

Scripture References
Genesis 2-3 ♦ 1 Timothy 2:8-15 ♦ 2 Corinthians 11:3

Adam lived nine hundred and thirty years alongside his wife Eve who likewise lived a lengthy and prolific span. Imagine living for that long, parenting many children, surviving the best you can, with a vivid memory of a better time when people had no need of clothing or weaponry. It is hard for us to conceive of such perfect ease and harmony between man and nature. Picture the mournful memory of this existence in the shadow of losing beautiful fellowship with God and complete purity—an epoch now suspended by your own failure.

Adam and Eve's marriage began under the most idyllic of settings with God acting as the matchmaker for this first union. Their fall from this ideal has been the subject of philosophy, literature, and theology ever since. Their one act of defiance against their Creator is the cause of all sin, natural disaster, crime, deformity, disease, and depravity on this earth. This is where we and all our problems began; hence we need to understand everything we can about Eve's story and its many implications for us today.

A Mere Glance

Here is a brief and familiar synopsis of the first couple's disaster: Adam and Eve were created by a loving God who gave them everything they needed in order to be happy. They broke the one rule, hid from God, and had to answer for their sin. They were doomed to a life of toil and suffering with the hazy promise of a future redemption. Eve would have to submit to an imperfect leader and Adam would eat by the sweat of his brow. Eve would experience pain in childbirth and see one of her sons murder the other. Eve and Adam would live a life of toil outside of the garden and be responsible for populating the earth and enduring the consequences of sin. While this is an accurate recounting of what took place in Genesis, merely focusing on man's bad choices and the sequence of events can perpetuate a simplistic understanding of the origin of sin.

Much of the popular teaching and preaching of our day attributes evil and suffering to man's "free will" in answer to the question of why a loving and powerful God would allow evil into His Eden. This presupposes that God is somehow restrained by man's will. It is as if "free will" is to blame for everything man does and everything God can't do. If you are not satisfied with this small picture of God, then stay with me! Along with understanding the big picture is the challenge of identifying the original design of God's plan for man and woman. This original design or pattern was the target of Satan's scheme.

The Garden View
To get a better view than a mere recitation of the facts allow, let's look at the conditions into which Eve was created. We are told in Genesis 2:15 that Adam has been commissioned to tend the Garden of Eden. God has chosen to place Adam in a locale that will need continual cultivation. God also gives Adam the first negative command in verse 17, "you must not eat from the tree of the knowledge of good and evil, for when you eat of it you will surely die." There are two distinct trees in Genesis 2:9: the tree of good and evil and the tree of life, the latter carrying no restrictions for Adam.

In verse 18, God observes that the man is alone and should not remain so, yet he doesn't immediately provide the solution; He allows Adam to continue working in the garden. The man will tend the animals and give them all names. He will study the animal kingdom and see the one common denominator amongst the diverse species: sexual reproduction. He becomes more and more aware of his isolation. He alone of all the creation is left unable to procreate. Adam can only relate to the beasts on their terms. He knows no equal to himself. Apart from this Adam is completely fulfilled in his pre-fall relationship with God. He simply needs a wife to complete the family picture.

God already knows what Adam needs and gets busy with his final creation: a woman. She is made from Adam's very being, presented to him by God—and there is instant chemistry. The man said, "This is now bone of my bones and flesh of my flesh; she shall be called woman, for she was taken out of man." The woman was made from man, and the two become one again through sexual intercourse. Unlike the animals, the woman can relate to Adam on his level. Intellectually, emotionally, spiritually, and sexually, she is his match. At this point, Adam is satisfied with calling his woman according to what she is. Seeing her correctly as an extension of himself, perhaps he has overlooked her complexity. Or, perhaps Adam is so excited he's got other things on his mind! Speculation aside, Adam does not yet give her a name to signify who she is.

More importantly, a principle is established here which should not be overlooked: God creates the woman for man—not the other way around. This is the apostle Paul's interpretation of the creative order in I Corinthians 11:8-9, "For man did not come from woman, but woman from man; neither was man created for woman, but woman for man." In our distorted world this principle is hard to swallow, but for pre-fall Adam and his woman it was good! "The man and his wife were both naked, and they felt no shame." [Gen.:5]

See Adam's beautiful exclamation of delight in knowing that this exquisitely feminine creature comes from him in verse 3. In the New Living Translation he cries, "At last!" Whatever amount of time Adam had to live without a wife, must have felt like an eternity to him. He has longed for her. Her life comes from him. She will not only be his helper in childbearing and his work, but also a constant reminder of his value to God. As far as identity goes, Adam still only understands (my speculation) his wife for what she is. Who she is, is yet to be defined. Their time together before the fall may have been short lived. The two are equally valued and wanted by the Creator. They are equal in essence, but do not have the same exact roles or responsibilities. The most important thing to note is the creative order which suggests that Adam is meant to lead his wife and that she should turn to him for direction and protection. Since we are told that they felt no shame, it seems that the Woman was not bothered by her husband's leadership or headship before sin!

Adam's Unbeatable Rival
The trouble begins in Genesis 3 when the woman starts listening to the "serpent." In the Hebrew the word rendered "serpent" is Nachash which means a shining one. Elsewhere in the Bible, Saraph, Hebrew for burning one, is used interchangeably with Nachash. The Genesis account as a whole is meant to be interpreted as historical narrative. Figures of speech are used throughout Scripture to call attention to a truth and reality that cannot be adequately conveyed with what is literal. Hence, "serpent," I believe, could possibly be figurative for a "celestial being" or "shining spirit-being." This fits the description of Satan described in 2 Corinthians 11:3-14 as a beguiler disguised as an angel of light. Ezekiel 8 gives much detail as to the beauty and wisdom with which God created his most brilliant angel, Lucifer, and the angel's pride which caused God to cast him out of his presence. [For more information regarding this interpretation see the notes and appendices of E.W. Bullinger's, The Companion Bible.]

The evil force at work in the garden is Satan himself, the master of deception and disguise, in full brilliant splendor. Notice that Satan goes straight to the Woman. He acts quickly to prevent the woman from understanding who she really is. Just like the first woman, we today are very susceptible to lies and frauds when we don't appreciate who we are in light of who our Creator is. The woman is intrigued by the glorious shining being. He will cause her to doubt everything she knows about God. He will cause her vision of Adam to pale in comparison to his own luster. She will be misled by the serpent's suggestions and give it a listening ear. Does she turn in alarm to her husband? No, she rather likes the indecent suggestion that something is being withheld from her! Words cannot adequately convey the power of Satan's seduction over the woman.

It is here in these verses that there is a peculiar silence from Adam. His wife is conversing with the lying, deceiving, though beautiful, celestial being, and all alone in her defense of God's law—a law to which she is fairly new. A law (cf. Gen. 3:3) which she cannot even quote accurately! There is no response from Adam, no intervention, no warning, no visible effort to protect her from the serpent's lies. Nothing! Where was Adam?

He was right there! Genesis 3:6 is a most infuriating verse: "When the woman saw that the fruit of the tree was good for food and pleasing to the eye, and also desirable for gaining wisdom, she took some and ate it. She also gave some to her husband, who was with her, and he ate it." It seems Adam passively stood by while his wife was under attack. He was the one to whom God had given the command not to eat of this tree. He was more knowledgeable and experienced than his woman. The woman who had not yet even received a name! It seems that Adam was stunned into silence.

The woman entertained wisdom from someone other than her husband. Her sin is not just about believing Satan's lies, but in violating a very beneficial order already established by God. In fact, Adam unwittingly assists in this role reversal by remaining passive. Then he partakes of the fruit at her offer and together they become aware of their sin. They try in vain to cover their nakedness. The nakedness which was meant by God to facilitate their oneness has become a source of shame. They are veritable innocents at odds with nature. But they do know enough to feel guilty and hide from God. Adam and his woman are faced with the unbearable realization of their own nakedness and failure.

Innocence Lost
The couple's relationship will never return to honeymoon bliss. Because of their disobedience they will constantly be aware of sin and shame. Man will blame his wife for burdening and misleading him and she will struggle to respect a man who hesitates or refuses to defend her. Their perceptions of each other are distorted by sin and all of their progeny carry the scars.

In 3:8 we see that Adam and the woman are no longer at ease in the presence of God. As the Lord God walks in the garden the man and his wife hide from God among the trees of the garden. Their life of freedom and intimacy with God has been forever altered. The Creator holds the man accountable first. When God calls out to Adam, "Where are you?" the man's answer is gut wrenching in light of his former innocence. "I heard you in the garden, and I was afraid because I was naked, so I hid." When asked "Who told you were naked? Have you eaten of the tree that I commanded you not to eat from?" Adam is devastated by his own guilt and shame. Without having experienced Adam's former communion with God it is impossible for us to fully appreciate the depths of his despair after sinning.

I believe Adam's bitter answer honestly reveals his distorted perspective. God's gift to him, the woman, gave him the fruit. In other words, "She's to blame, I was in a position I could not help or avoid." In these words is the beginning of all marital discord. All of the abuse and passive aggression from Man to Wife, and everything sinful in between, is captured in Adam's bitter words. God then says to the woman, "What is this you have done?" The answer is factual, "The serpent deceived me and I ate." So the Lord God begins to curse the serpent, but first we will look at a couple of issues.

Bare Naked Reality
God knew what would happen in advance. He is all knowing! He was not truly ignorant of Adam's whereabouts or the cause of his shame. He knew and continues to know everything before it happens. Would you dare to go against conventional thought and reason through this with me?

The common explanation for the presence of sin in the garden is that God wanted mankind to have a choice. This is partly based on an assumption with which I do agree: God is completely sovereign and in control! This naturally begs the question: why allow the choice to be made in the first place? Many have come to believe, or assume, God allowed his creation to make a choice because of the value He places on our choosing. There is this assumption in much of contemporary evangelicalism regarding "free will" that is not supported in the text. In fact, in the creation account we see nothing about God presenting "choices" in the modern sense of the word. We see the opposite—an ultimatum: "But you must not eat from the tree of the knowledge of good and evil for when you eat of it you will surely die…." (Gen. 2:17)

It is the latecomer Eve who initially chooses. The garden was not set up for man to make choices on his own, but rather to consult with his Creator. God's design was that man would come to him to find out what was good. Alas, choice is placed on a pedestal by man's presumption, not God or the Bible. But God is too compassionate to really leave us to our own devices. He knows that apart from His grace we would never be able to make any good moves or choices. He also knows that mankind is no match for the fallen Lucifer, also known as Satan. His grace is necessary because there is no excuse for sin, even for the outmatched Adam and his woman. Perhaps what God is illustrating for us in Genesis is the complete hopelessness of human choice and initiative.

The Big Picture
For reasons known only to God, the shining, brilliant, fallen Satan was allowed into the garden. The woman was exposed to

his lies and fell for his seduction. Having been tempted by her every sense, the woman offers the same to her husband. On the surface, and in accordance with many years of pop-Christianity, it may seem that because man has perverted God's perfect world—now God must come up with "plan B." When one looks at our world, the fingerprints of Adam's sin are everywhere. When one reads Paul's word in Romans 5:1, it is also clear that while "Adam trespassed and passed condemnation onto us"—God has it all under control with Jesus and His free offer of the Gospel. As Adam is no match for Satan, Satan's deceptive power is no match for God's redemptive power. I believe God's redemptive power was put in place before it was needed! I find it much more attributive of God's absolute sovereignty to see the entrance of sin as certainly displeasing to Him, but within His will.

A frequently asked question in a society that believes everyone can come up with his own definition of love is: "If God is loving and just, then why does He subject his creation to sin and suffering?" My answer which is not original to me is this: "For the sake of his glory!" This means that His love must be seen in the context of his glory. To God, His own glory is everything and permeates every iota of Holy Scripture. Everything else is secondary to God's passion for His glory. "The nations will fear the name of the Lord, all the kings of the earth will revere your glory."(Ps. 10:15) The consequences of man's choice will be devastating to man and grievous to the heart of God. But even sinful choices and actions are meant by God to bring about His will. God's ultimate goal is to bring glory to Himself. When He demonstrates his wrath—or when He disciplines us—this is true. When he forgives us, this is true. His ultimate reason for everything is poignantly conveyed in Isaiah 48:11, "For my own sake, for my own sake, I do it, for how should my name be profaned? My glory I will not give to another."

As much as Adam must already have witnessed of God's glory in creation, he will now learn about God's sovereign grace. It is for this reason that God pursues Adam after he sins. It is because of

God's sovereign grace that God extracts a confession from the two and gives them the low-down on their sin and its consequences. He does the same for us. He makes those he pursues aware of their sin. He shows us our own responsibility. He corrects our misunderstanding of his Word, and he sets the record straight. But he doesn't leave it at that! He also sets the stage for his grace to change our lives.

So, one might say, the story is not primarily about Adam, Eve, and their sin. It is crucial to the plot, but their need for forgiveness is not the bottom line. God could have prevented the whole thing in the first place! The real story pivots on God's desire to demonstrate His glory and bring his creation into it! The original sin is not a derailment from God's plot. Satan is the originator of sin, but God has his own purposes for permitting Satan this role as the tempting serpent, or glorious, shining deceiver.

Cursed is the Ground

God lays heavy blame on the serpent for the deception of the woman and promises vindication for the woman and her offspring. Even if Adam and Eve were not able to understand the vast implications of the seed of the woman crushing the serpent's head (Gen. 3:15), the promise of salvation through a coming Messiah is there for us to grasp. This is another figure of speech which means that one day all of Satan's schemes and purposes will be destroyed by Jesus.

God's sermon to the woman is often misunderstood to be God's new definition of the woman's life. This is not meant to be a model, rather a matter of fact preview of her new life with the consequences of sin. The model for Adam and the woman was before sin. The original pattern and order is not cancelled. God's words to the woman are simply a preview of her new life in a world made sinful.

> To the woman he said, "I will greatly increase your pains in childbearing; with pain you will give birth to children. Your

desire will be for your husband, and he will rule over you."
To Adam he said, "Because you listened to your wife and ate from the tree about which I commanded you, 'You must not eat of it,' Cursed is the ground because of you; through painful toil you will eat of it all the days of your life. It will produce thorns and thistles for you and you will eat the plants of the field. By the sweat of your brow you will eat your food until you return to the ground, since from it you were taken; for dust you are and to dust you will return." *Genesis 3:16-19*

Increased pains in childbearing are obviously not a pleasant aspect of womanhood, but this is not necessarily a curse. Reasonably so, Eve's sinful state will handicap her ability to cope with pain. But suffering will build character and caution into her psyche. One take on the reference to "desire" is that in spite of the pain of childbearing woman will be motivated to procreate by the desire or longing for her husband referred to in 3:16. This is undoubtedly true since God created woman with this desire for her husband and in spite of the fall she still possesses it. The root meaning for "desire" is associated with the same use of this word in Genesis 4:7 when God warns Cain of the sin that "desires" to master him. God's warning to the woman is for all of us to hear because it still rings true today. On one hand it is undeniably true that woman will have the sexual desire for her husband which facilitates procreation and family life. On the other hand, that same desire will always be tainted by varying degrees of a female propensity for deception and control over men—which is really the main point. Unflattering as it is, this is a necessary caution to us who must live with the perpetual tension between healthy desire and sinful perversion of what God intended between husbands and wives.

The Bottom Line
In God's sermon to Adam and the woman he addresses two pre-fall concepts that will now be distorted by sin: submission as it

relates to the woman's relationship with her husband, and work as it relates to the man's calling and purpose in life. Simply put, Woman will still be under the order God established by creating Adam first, but she will now have to submit as a sinful woman to a sinful man. By the same token, Man will still work, not in the perfect and supple garden, but on cursed ground with painful toil. Understanding Adam's sermon is not as difficult. Yet, his consequences are probably more agonizing than the woman's. As a Christian woman, I recognize that the role of leader, if seen as that of sacrificial headship, is harder to bear than that of submissive woman. It is the man God holds most accountable.

The increased childbearing pain is simply due to the woman's new sinful state. Emotional and psychological focus will not come easily to women burdened with a sinful nature. However, when childbirth pains are positively viewed as a natural process and the birth is progressing normally, many women throughout the ages have felt a strong connection and reliance upon God during labor. My speculation is that God is warning his creation of the difficulty sin will make of the intense physical and emotional nature of procreation.

Even though natural childbirth is not for every woman, when we as women aren't in such a modern rush to alleviate pain, we can see what women of by gone eras experienced: the pain of childbearing points us to grace. It is not surprising that many women despise or at least misunderstand one of the best physical reminders we have of our importance to God. God becomes a man through a woman! Eve's progeny will lead up to the eventual birth of God's Son. Birth pains continue to remind us of the price Jesus paid for our redemption! By that token, pain can be valuable.

The reference to "pain in childbearing" is also symbolic of the woman's role of mothering. There are many aspects of mothering, besides childbirth itself, that are painful and beset by sin. Nevertheless, this is still to be the primary role of woman.

Immutable Principles
On another level there is a very challenging issue here. As women, we have many longings for meaningful relationships, home, intimacy with a man, and nurturing. We often see men as the fulfillment of these dreams. A single woman can find all of her longings met in the person of Jesus. Our God is husband to the widow and father to the fatherless. Those who are not married need not wait for a man to complete them. Every child of God is complete in Christ regardless of marital status or success!

For those of us who are married, the reality of marriage can be frustrating. Women do need direction and leadership from their husbands. Not because we are inferior, but because God designed us to complement each other in our roles. God's grace is the defining principle in marriage roles. Yet, it is difficult for husbands to hear their orders from God if a lot of nagging comes from the wife. Even justified protests will fall on deaf ears when a man (remember the effects of sin) feels threatened or disrespected by his woman. It is a wise woman who prays and uses sparingly her gift of verbal expression. Our silence leaves room for God's voice to be heard! A submissive woman understands this. She lovingly serves her husband and lets him see her joy in doing so. In our culture this will get any man's attention! In the meantime, the legitimate need for protection, leadership, and guidance must be met in Christ.

In 1 Timothy 2:11-15 we see an unchanging principle established by God which has little to do with equality or culture:

> "Let a woman learn quietly with all submissiveness. I do not permit a woman to teach or to exercise authority over a man; rather, she is to remain quiet. For Adam was formed first, then Eve; and Adam was not deceived, but the woman was deceived and became a transgressor. Yet she will be saved through childbearing—if they continue in faith and love and holiness, with self-control."

Some women are actually offended by this passage. God means it as a blessing to woman that despite sin, she will still be entrusted with the divine role of mothering.

Role Reversal
In creation, the role of woman is very simple—a life giving helper to her husband. Her work depends on his calling. Her calling is her man! Her talents are launched and culminated in the calling of mothering children and nurturing her family. Despite sin, this is true for woman. Childbearing—or all the things that involve mothering, nurturing, life-giving, loving, building, creating, and encouraging- is her consolation prize. Regardless of sin or history, woman is given these things as her challenge. Even though her role is simple, woman herself is much more complex in character than her role suggests. She brings richness and depth of character to her calling as life giver. The same could be said for us, Eve's daughters.

In light of this and all the biblical implications of God's creative pattern, what should Eve have been doing in the garden instead of talking to the serpent? She should have turned to Adam. She could have looked to him for direction. She was created with a special vulnerability that requires her husband's protection. Biblically and emotionally, male/female role reversals are usually disastrous. Adam should have been the leader, told off the serpent, and fought for his woman. Today in our culture we are faced with the same dilemma as Eve: Should I believe the cunning lies of the world which say that I am entitled to much more than God has promised? In the recesses of my heart do I secretly worship something other than God himself? Or should I turn to the husband God has given me and join him in meekness? Even more, do we Christians have clarity about what we reject when we stray from God's original design for men and women?

The many wounds of our culture and the ravages of sin often exhaust our men, just as the impressive serpent/Satan must have overwhelmed Adam. Sometimes wives must wait for men to become true spiritual leaders. Until that day comes, find life and comfort in God Himself. A less than ideal marriage or marital failure does not doom a woman to second class citizenship in heaven! We women can find our life in Christ through Christian sisterhood, prayer, and service. But the highest calling for wives is to lovingly submit to our husbands as unto the Lord. As I Peter 3 says, our submission is modeled after that of Jesus when His enemies hurled insults at Him! As Jesus was treated unfairly, so we can expect some aspects of womanhood to be unfair. Even in the midst of marital discord women can bring glory to God! In the meantime, the role of the primary spiritual leader of the home is not very cushy and often least desired by men themselves.

Thwarted Leadership
I am prone to react harshly to Adam's passivity while his wife was being seduced by the devil. On this side of heaven it is impossible for us to really know what went wrong within Adam or Eve. Scripture does not tell us explicitly. But there is an undeniable connection between their disobedience and our own modern day marital failures. Let's put ourselves as eyewitnesses in the garden and see how well we can identify with Adam's frustrated leadership.

The beauty of the woman takes Adam's breath away. She comes from him and has been given to him to bear his children! They now have each other and perfect fellowship with God. They can freely express their mutual love, wonder, and desire. The woman can relate to him on his level and understand his work and help him. During their brief time together he has explained the essentials of living in Eden. They can eat anything except from the tree of knowledge of good and evil. Adam directs her away from that tree. There is no need for that fruit anyway; all they need comes directly from God! The man and his wife explore the garden as he shows her the many responsibilities he has been given. But the woman is drawn to the forbidden tree, where the shining being waits with cunning words.

Imagine the shock and paralysis of Adam when he realizes that his woman is entranced by the great deceiver. Doesn't she remember what he told her? Hasn't his love meant anything to her? Is she not satisfied with his wisdom and the role God has designed for her? Why not look to him for the truth! Oh! this woman who seemed so intoxicating is now rejecting him for the most impressive of all God's creation. What a blow to the man's sense of strength. Adam knows she is being deceived. Why can't he speak or cry out a warning? "Oh, woman," his heart moans, "you were made for me, why do you believe the serpent's lies?" Her eyes are on the tree and her hands reach out greedily for the fruit. Stunned, Adam watches helplessly as she eats and pleasantly offers the fruit to him. He deliberately eats of it and knows instantly of their sin.

Perhaps Adam simply could not rise above his own wounded, thwarted ego. Maybe we women are meant to come down hard on the pride and arrogance of Eve for believing the manipulations of a beautiful imposter who told her what she wanted to hear! I believe our sympathies should be with Adam who could not compete with an angelic, though fallen, being. Are you guilty of comparing your husband to out of reach celebrities and icons whose brilliance is unattainable? Do you, like Eve, proudly believe that you are entitled to more than what you already have? Are you willing to throw away your blessings for something that may well turn out to be a curse?

We are really no different from the first woman. And like Eve, we must face life's challenges, albeit complicated by our own sin, and find a way to be life givers. The two sinners will be clothed by the Lord God himself and driven away from their sumptuous life in the garden. God protects Adam from further anguish by sealing off the garden and banishing them from it. Ironically, they had to be driven away from the life they destroyed for themselves! They had to submit to a continual reminder of God's judgment every time they saw the cherubim and flaming sword which God placed at the entrance to Eden. This is compassionate punishment from the Creator who knows that Adam can no longer eat of the tree of life now that he has eaten from the forbidden fruit. Immortality in the fallen, sinful state would be unbearable. In not destroying the tree of life God leaves Adam and all mankind with a hint of a better future. But Adam and Eve would not know the kind of victory we are promised in Christ Jesus.

The Mystery Revealed
For many thousands of years God's prophets understood that marriage is symbolic of something holy. But the mystery of its symbolism remained unknown except to perhaps a select few. In Ephesians 5:31-3 Paul exults in the mystery finally revealed in Christ: "For this reason a man will leave his father and mother and be united to his wife, and the two will become one flesh. This is a profound mystery, but I am talking about Christ and the church." Now Paul points out that biblical marriage illustrates that which exists through Christ and the church. Husbands are to model their headship after the sacrificial love of Christ for his bride the church. Our men need major prayer support and discipleship to live up to this! Women are designed to portray the loving submission of the Bride of Christ, the Church, to her Head: Jesus Christ. We women need major prayer and mentoring to accomplish this! Through the Gospel this mystery has now been revealed, not made completely understandable and politically correct, not made culturally popular; just a mystery revealed by the complementary roles of man and woman.

When Adam heard God speak of the serpent's head being crushed, was he at least a little intrigued? Could he have held to that promise as reason enough to continue the struggle of life outside the garden? He must have fallen into despair and depression over his failure for at least some of his nine hundred and thirty years. But for this one moment Adam displays hope when he turns to his wife and names her Eve, Mother of Life. By naming his wife, it is as if Adam is acting as leader and saying to Eve, "I believe in God's power and promises, He has not abandoned us! This life will be painful and toilsome, but we will trust in the Creator together. We will accept whatever he gives us! We will tell our children of his loving laws."

The First Family—Genesis 4
Adam and Eve lived many centuries with their own failures. They had much heartbreak and disappointment as spouses and parents who had not lived up to God's ideal. When Adam and Eve began having children they were blessed with Cain and then Abel. It was Cain who seethed with sinful anger toward his brother Abel whose offering to God was truly righteous. He would not learn from his younger brother or consult his parents about his resentment. Nor did he listen when God warned him that his pride would be his downfall. Who of us can imagine the anguish that would have been Eve's when her younger son was martyred by the older. So soon after sin's entrance to the world, the first man to be murdered is killed by his own older brother simply for his purity. This is what Eve and her husband let loose in the world. But they kept going even when their offending son had to be exiled.

They kept giving life and multiplying in obedience to God. God blessed their continued union with another son, Seth, to take the place of their loss. Their prospects with God were unchanged, though every sin brought them greater and greater anguish. In the rock-strewn, sin infested world they shaped, the first man and woman clung to whatever remnant of his glory they could still see and cultivate in his creation. Man and woman passed on to their progeny the knowledge of God, the holy, loving, and merciful Creator who spared their lives. Their children would be able to know God under the same challenging conditions. They knew that in spite of their sin tarnished lives, they were not completely removed from God's will or protection. Seth is a reminder of God's constant gift of children for Man and Woman to raise in a family of faithfulness to God.

The Continual Reenactment
The essential point in all this is not our sin, but God's sovereign grace and glory. As we understand the nature of the first sin, we can see the same script from the garden of old reenacted today in our culture. There is an evil deceiver and destroyer who blinds our eyes to the glory of God revealed in marriage. Satan's goal of thwarting God's glory is best executed by messing up the distinct roles God has created man and woman to enjoy. The earth may be tainted, our sinful nature irreparable, but what God has established in marriage is still reflective of his glory because of his grace. Satan saw this from the beginning. Still today he goes after women with this covert strategy of enticing us away from the beautiful submission for which God created women. He uses many brilliant, glossy, temptations to strike a blow at the loving headship for which God created men. Men and women in our society are increasingly confused and misled about their roles and rewarded with anger and emptiness.

The message of Eve's life is surprising to me. Our lives and stories are about so much more than our failures and successes. All the good and bad in our lives are ultimately a springboard from which God will demonstrate to the world his sovereign grace. Through the gospel of Jesus Christ we can return to the beautiful design God has for women that our lives and marriages will truly reflect the loving submission of the Bride to her head: Christ. Says the psalmist, "The Mighty One, God the Lord, speaks and summons the earth from the rising of the sun to its setting." (Ps. 60:1) His soft cadences of love and mercy are orchestrating through every facet of life; leading, guiding, wooing women back to Him. Our human history begins with the entrance to Eden sealed off, but our future lies in knowing that through Jesus' blood sacrifice we will someday be allowed into the new Eden, where our lives will be glorified. God will save the garden for another time and place!

"He who has an ear, let him hear what the Spirit says to the churches. To him who overcomes, I will give the right to eat from the tree of life, which is in the paradise of God."

Revelation 2:7

Questions for Study and Discussion:

1. In terms of "pattern of creation" suggested by the text in Genesis 2 and 3, what is the implication for marriage as originally designed by God? If you disagree that there is a pattern please explain using scripture.

2. Genesis makes very clear that Man and Woman are both created in the image of God. How does this make male and female equal in importance and value to God?

3. What role does grace (as in God's pursuit of Adam) play in the choices we make? Can you describe the work of God's Sovereign Grace in your own life?

4. What is your response to the teaching of Paul in 1 Timothy 2:8-15? What is positive or negative about this for you personally?

5. What might be the challenges men face in trying to be strong leaders in a day and age of feminism and male bashing?

6. Read Genesis 2:19-25. In this account of God's creation of the woman and marriage, what details do you see as being vital to God's plan for marriage?

7. List any red flags you see in the dialogue between the woman and the serpent in Genesis 3:1-4.

8. Read Genesis 1:27-30; and 2:15. Before sin entered the picture, God gave Adam a job in the garden and a role as husband. How would these be affected according to Gen. 3:17-19?

9. Read Genesis 1:28-29 and 2:18. Prior to her sin, Eve was created with a special purpose. How would this purpose be affected by sin? (cf. Gen. 3:15-16)

10. Genesis 3:15 is the first prophecy of the Messiah. What hope does this offer mankind?

2

MARY—BLESSED AMONG WOMEN

Scripture References
Luke 1:1-5, John the Baptist
Luke 1:26-38, Mary visited by Gabriel
Luke 1:39-56, Mary visits Elizabeth, The Magnificat
Matt. 1:25, No physical union between Mary and Joseph until birth of Jesus
Matt. 1:2-17, Genealogy of Jesus Christ
Luke 3:23-38, Genealogy of Jesus Christ
Luke 2:1-7, Birth of Jesus in a stable
Luke 2:8-20, The shepherds and the angels
Luke 2:25, Simeon's praise for Jesus
John 1:1-18, The Word made flesh
John 1:19-34, John the Baptists' mission and baptism of Jesus
John 1:35-51, Jesus calls the Twelve
John 2:1-11, Wedding in Cana
John 2:12-25, Jesus at the temple in Jerusalem
Mark 3:31, His mother and brothers arrive
Matt. 12:46, They seek to speak to Him
Luke 8:19-21, Jesus has brothers and sisters?
Mark 3:20-21, Jesus' family fears He is going out of his mind
Acts 26:24, Paul accused of insanity when on trial
John 19:26, Mary stood near the cross of Jesus
John 19:23-30, Roman soldiers at crucifixion and Mary and John nearby
Isaiah 9:6, Description of the coming Messiah
Isaiah 53, The sacrificial Lamb expected by Jews
Acts 1:14, Mary and Jesus' brothers with the disciples after the ascension
Luke 11:27, Jesus responds to blessing upon His mother

Mary: Blessed Among Women—The Coming Messiah
In Genesis 3:15 God curses the serpent with this prophecy: "I will put enmity between you and the woman, and between your offspring and her offspring; he shall bruise your head, and you shall bruise his heel." Christian theologians consider those words to be prophetic of Christ's sacrificial death. Prophecies like Isaiah 7:14, written centuries before the New Testament, proclaimed "Behold, a virgin shall conceive and bear a son, and shall call his name Immanuel." Israel, the nation of refugees God continually preserved through wars, famines, rebellions, captivities, and dispersion, would one day see the birth of a Messiah. The Suffering Servant prophesied by Isaiah would be "despised and rejected by men; a man of sorrows and acquainted with grief...." One of the recurring themes of Jewish history and biblical narrative is the coming of the long awaited Messiah: The One who would save his people from their sins.

He would be a king like his ancestor David who prophesied of the resurrection of God's Son in Psalm 16:10: "For you will not abandon my soul to Sheol, or let your holy one see corruption." He would be a leader, a teacher, a servant, a healer, a prophet, a king—a savior. Of these promises every Jewish believer was taught. But what did these words mean? Who and what is Messiah? Was there a consensus among Jews concerning the coming of a Messiah or Savior? Though interpretations of prophecy varied depending on traditions of one's local rabbi or political party affiliation, faithful Jews everywhere longed for Messiah and raised their children on messianic prophecies. The Jews of this region described in the Gospels were much more legalistic and than their brothers in other parts of the Hellenized world. Their fear of history repeating itself led them to varying degrees of separatism and fear of the Gentile world.

Rome regarded Herod as a talented and effective administrator. He envisioned and orchestrated the rebuilding of the Jewish temple that had been desecrated and destroyed by pagan conquerors. He knew how to placate the population and manipulate the various sects and political parties. He brought Roman roads, peace, and commerce to the Palestinian region of his day. By Roman standards of order and efficiency he was known as Herod the Great. From a moral perspective Herod was an evil tyrant. He murdered his political enemy Hyrcanus; he murdered his own wife Mariamne and their two sons; and from his deathbed ordered the execution of Antipater, a son by another wife. In Scripture, Herod is notorious for his slaughter of the so-called "innocents" out of fear that he would be usurped by the baby reported by the Magi to be King of the Jews. Apparently, Herod's cruel competence as an administrator of Roman interests was enough to satisfy Augustus, who himself was not known for cruelty.

The Land of Israel
The world into which Jesus was born was rife with fear, political factions, legalism, and power struggles between rulers and leaders, both pagan and Jewish. The three most important institutions to the average Jew living in Palestine would have been: first, home and family, in which the mother taught and passed on important traditions and practices within the home; the local synagogue, in which men were the leaders and their sons the recipients of teaching from the learned rabbis and scribes; and the temple, in which was carried out the most sacred observances of the Hebrew people.

The Sanhedrin, the ruling council and Supreme Court of the Jews, proclaimed themselves the buffer between Herod and the Jewish people. But in fact the high priest and other members of the Council were very much in league with Herod. In Scripture, Jesus himself never criticized Roman government or its leaders. He was criticized for his friendliness with Matthew and other tax collectors and he encouraged people to pay their taxes. His focus was on eternal salvation and the kingdom of God. It was the Jewish political and religious leaders who were his enemies and were most oppressive of their own people.

The Rescue Mission

Matthew 1:17 summarizes the history of God's people and their long wait for Messiah: forty two generations from Abraham to the Christ. In the all knowing wisdom of God this was the time and place for sending Messiah. So, to the city of Nazareth in Galilee God sent his angel Gabriel to find a maiden named Mary, who by God's providence was betrothed to a man named Joseph. Perhaps as Mary went about her daily routine she took joy in thinking about her betrothed, Joseph, whose genealogy is outlined in Matthew 1 as the house of King David. On that day she might have been sewing the very clothes and linens that young women would carry into marriage. Possibly Mary was alone with God, deep in prayer and worship. Whatever her tasks or location, Mary was the one whom the angel visited. Her simple world was never to be the same again.

Why Mary? Mary had many qualities that we will see as we study her life, but there was one main qualification which led her to be visited by the angel Gabriel. Luke 3:23 begins the genealogy of Christ through Mary's family. She and Joseph were qualified by their lineage as descendants of King David to be the parents of the Messiah. Even the step father, Joseph, would need to be in fulfillment of the Davidic lineage. He and Mary were living testaments to the sovereign power of God over history.

The ancient prophecies of Judaism were the bread and butter of every faithful Jew's life. Children went to schools held by rabbis and in the home mothers taught children psalms, hymns, and songs filled with messianic prophecies. In many Jewish communities, including those of the ultra conservative Palestinian region, girls and boys learned to read and write in the home or local synagogue. Boys who showed promise would receive extensive training in Torah, no matter their intended trade or profession. The Jews of the New Testament were a people of The Book. They took seriously and debated the meaning of prophecies. Minute detail was paid to every nuance of the law. Mothers worked furiously to end the week with a beautiful Shabbat (Sabbath) dinner filled with ritual blessings and traditions used to teach God's word to children. Children were encouraged to ask pertinent questions at meals. Major portions of Scripture and Bible stories were committed to memory and told and retold around the family firelight. Mary must have lived in such a home. She must have dreamed of continuing those traditions with Joseph.

When Mary was visited by the angel Gabriel (Matthew 1:18; Luke 1:27-38) she asked a pertinent question. In response to the angel's announcement that she would conceive and bear the Son of God, Mary asked in Luke 1:34, "How will this be, since I am a virgin?" Mary doesn't doubt the words of the angel concerning the favor and blessing bestowed upon her, she is merely practical. Mary wants to know how this prophecy from the angel will match up with reality as she knows it. After all, she is not yet married and has been nothing but chaste. Amazingly, Mary is satisfied with Gabriel's answer: God's Holy Spirit will cause the pregnancy and the Holy One to be born will be God's Son.

Gabriel goes on to say in Luke 1:35 that the "Holy Spirit will come upon you, and the power of the Most High will overshadow you; therefore the child to be born will be called holy—the Son of God." After such tremendous prophecy Mary must have found great comfort in hearing reference to her cousin Elizabeth and knowing that she would not be alone in this. There is a dual miracle taking place, she would take courage in the work God had already begun within Elizabeth. Even though Mary trusted God and believed his promises, how could she have understood the full implications of it all? Most of us are naïve when we first become wives and mothers under ordinary circumstances!

Mary's Humility

Many things in Luke 1 and 2 stand out to me about Mary's character. The initial thing to see in Mary is that she is very humble. From a practical and spiritual standpoint her life has just been invaded by the Holy Spirit! She has seen an angelic being from whom she has been given news about which she has no choice and which will bring scandal and inconvenience to her family! She will undoubtedly be stigmatized by this pregnancy! She will be put away by her fiancé! She will not have the wedding for which every Jewish maiden longs! Yet Mary says to Gabriel, "Behold, I am the servant of the Lord, let it be to me according to your word."

There is no indication in Scripture that Mary comes from a poor family, nor that Joseph and his families are deprived. They were probably from hardworking and modestly successful families. This would be in keeping with the godly priorities of honesty, hard work, and excellence held by God's people. The most sensible thing to assume about Mary's background is that she had a great life planned. She would be married to a wonderful and respected man who would be a good provider and leader. Her parents were probably very proud of her. At this point Joseph would be working hard in anticipation of bringing home a bride to his family home. In other words, Mary's life wasn't going from bad to worse. She probably wasn't a desperate farm laborer or impoverished maiden getting married to a poor carpenter. She was betrothed to a man of spiritually noble lineage, with a profitable trade, and respect in the Jewish community.

And yet "I am the servant of the Lord" sums up her self identity, even when her future is jeopardized. Mary has a sense of humility based on a high view of God's sovereignty. She has something better than self-esteem. This young maiden seems to be way ahead of many educated and emancipated women in their thirties. How many of us can have our very lives invaded and enthusiastically chalk it all up to servanthood? Mary has God-esteem! She finds her identity in God. She can take that identity with her anywhere, under any circumstances. There is something deeper within Mary than mere acquiescence to God's will. She is joyfully humble. She loves God and his will. She feels favored and blessed to be a part of his will! Did the Holy One of Israel orchestrate Joseph's choice of bride in favor of Mary for her depth of humility?

Mary's Passion
I believe for Mary, and all of us, it is a high view of God's sovereignty that gives us a healthy view of ourselves. Mary was brought up on the Scriptures of her people. Her faith was based on the historical narratives, poetry, and prophecy meticulously inscribed and preserved by men of God throughout the ages. Her humility was not based on allegedly humble circumstances, but on a very educated and informed sense of God's greatness. But she wasn't going to try to handle everything on her own. She needed a godly woman to turn to. She needed to see how God was working out his miraculous plan. We are told in Luke 1:29 that when Mary was greeted by the angel her reaction was "greatly troubled and amazed." We don't know from Scripture if Mary tells her parents anything, though it is likely she did. It is hard to picture parents allowing a maiden to make a three day journey to the hills of Judea without an escort of some kind.

It is doubtful that such a godly woman as Mary would cause her parents alarm and distress by leaving home without explaining something. Perhaps she told them only about the angel's words concerning Elizabeth. They might have hired a cart to take her. Or maybe her parents accompanied her and wanted her to see Elizabeth to validate the prophecies. In Luke 1:39 we are told that "in those days Mary arose and went with haste into the hill country, to a town in Judah, and she entered the house of Zechariah and greeted Elizabeth."

I like to imagine that Mary was traveling either with her parents or a trusted family friend as an escort. I can see her riding her favorite donkey—a gentle mare loved and petted by Mary since her girlhood. On the long journey Mary is quiet except for her own thoughts and occasional praying and singing of psalms out loud. She might have been trotting along on sheer adrenaline yearning to pour out her heart of praise with Elizabeth. Her first goal would be to see Elizabeth! To get confirmation from her cousin that what she heard from the angel is true. I picture Mary ostensibly calm and restrained, yet teeming with an intense desire to not just pray or worship in the ordinary sense. Mary would have wanted to see Elizabeth so that together they could revel in God's glory!

Mary's journey to see Elizabeth was an act of faith. Whether she traveled alone or with family she went to see the pregnant and past childbearing Elizabeth. When she arrived at the house of Zechariah and greeted Elizabeth, and Elizabeth heard the greeting of Mary, the baby leaped in Elizabeth's womb. Luke 1:41-45 explains that Elizabeth was filled with the Holy Spirit and exclaimed prophetic words, "Blessed are you among women, and blessed is the fruit of your womb! And why is this granted to me that the mother of my Lord should come to me? For behold, when the sound of your greeting came to my ears, the baby in my womb leaped for joy. And blessed is she who believed that there would be a fulfillment of what was spoken to her from the Lord."

We don't know from Scripture how well acquainted Mary was with Elizabeth. Elizabeth seems surprised to see Mary. Mary's pilgrimage to see the pregnant Elizabeth was fruitful! How strange and glorious it must have been for her to hear Elizabeth's cry of delight and prophecy! Elizabeth was the proof of God's promises. Her son would be the forerunner of Jesus the Messiah. Similarly, her miracle was the preview to Mary of God's promised Son.

To us, Elizabeth represents the mature and godly woman who has had spiritual and emotional victory in her life. She is a beacon of hope to others who need to be affirmed in their faith and spiritual journey. Elizabeth is about faith encouragement. She is the older woman you know you can confide in. She is the one to whom we run when we need mothering and nurturing. Elizabeth has lived her life in faith and trust and is the one who recognizes that same thing in other women. Sometimes we need to carefully select an Elizabeth for ourselves. But in order for us to really experience the effect of this special womanly nurture, we must take our mentoring relationships to the next level. We can't settle for pleasant exchanges and note cards, though those are the place to start!

Mary Is a Poet of Worship Songs
We've got to see the power base of prayer and worship experienced by Mary and Elizabeth. Mary's response to Elizabeth was a response to God. Mary's poem of praise in Luke 1:46-55 is filled with Old Testament quotations and unrestrained reveling in God's glory. Her prayer of praise is thought by scholars to be based on Hannah's prayer in 1 Samuel when Hannah presents Samuel to the Lord. Her worship is founded on deep knowledge of God and his trajectory. It is rooted in a vision from his past workings for what he is continuing in history through her child, His Son! Mary and Elizabeth were not merely excited about a pregnancy. They were marveling at God's power. They were reveling in the supremacy of a God who keeps a vision for his glory alive in his people. A vision so strong that a loving mother would offer her son up to the Lord for the sake of God's glory. I would imagine that vibrant worship was a way of life for each of them. And their worship was compelling because they knew His ways.

Like Mary, we need to keep before us a picture of a God who is in control. A God worthy of the highest praise! This is especially true when circumstances don't seem very divine. When women of God become entranced by God we won't be lukewarm or merely obedient. We will love to obey God. This will show in our worship.

Healthy and Holy Obsession
Earlier when Elizabeth was quoted as blessing Mary for believing the promise of the Lord, we saw it resulted in worship. For Christian women who live by faith and not by sight, we should be caught up in a continual cycle of prayer and worship. Imagine women relating to each other through prayer and worship, not just ordinary conversation! Could it be that Mary and Elizabeth were strong because they practiced this already? Might this have been part of their Hebrew culture? Luke 1:56 tells us that Mary stayed with Elizabeth for about three months and then returned home. What did Mary do whenever she was reminded in some

way of the difficulty of her situation? How did she handle the uncertainty of her future? Just transport yourself to Mary's time and heart of faith.

God interrupts your life with the most earth shattering event in history. A heavenly being announces to you alone that you have been chosen to conceive, bear, and rear the Son of God. You don't know for sure who will support you or even believe you. The whole thing sounds bizarre to even the godliest people you know. Yet you know what the angel announced is perfectly in line with all the prophecies: Suffering Servant; Sacrificial Lamb; Wonderful Counselor; Mighty God; Everlasting Father; Prince of Peace; Immanuel; God is with us; born of a virgin! Who are you to try to dodge the will of the One True God? He has favored you! You are his hand maiden. Your whole life is about the Living God. He is all you have. What choice is there? So you pray to him and worship him through all these overwhelming circumstances! (cf. Isaiah 7, 9, and 53)

God is most glorified not by our obedience, but by the joyful attitude we display as we obey him during a time of suffering or challenge. Or through out a lifetime of suffering! The duty God requires of us is that we find our complete satisfaction and happiness in him. If we are truly obeying him out of love, we delight in obeying him. This doesn't happen automatically. It takes growth in prayer, worship, and discipline. It is when our actions, attitudes, and emotions are surrendered to him that we are reconciled to the conjoined emotional sense and biblical sense of God's word. Focusing on God and his word in worship is the vehicle for reconciling our emotions to God.

Apart from Jesus himself, I can think of no one else in Scripture who exhibits joyful surrender and satisfaction in God better than Mary. She is faced with stigma, scandal, and future suffering. Yet she feels blessed and happy to be "the hand maid of the Lord." This seems insane to the world. It is not good deeds or the ability to endure suffering that make Christ followers stand out in a sea of religious do gooders! It is our happiness to serve—our joy in what others call sacrifice—always rejoicing and giving thanks in all circumstances—and abstaining from evil that puts us in the God entranced cult of Jesus (I Thes. 5:16)! This is what perplexes the world around us. This is what Mary had that captivates Christians and non Christians alike. This is the same intensity that will repel some as well.

The Pondering Heart
As far as we know, Mary's main female confidante, other than perhaps her mother, was Elizabeth—a woman whose own godliness was well known and guaranteed to give Mary strength and affirmation. We networking, cell phoning, and emailing communicators could learn much from Mary's spiritual focus. She had a resolve seldom encouraged in today's church. She probably didn't surround herself with a camp of supporters who would speak on her behalf. She did do something so alien to our culture that we must really think hard to see what Scripture makes very clear! Just notice the trend in Mary's life.

In the account of the shepherd's visit to the baby Jesus, Luke 2:19 says that Mary's response to their adoration was to treasure up all these things and "ponder them in her heart." When Mary and Joseph took Jesus to the temple for his dedication and had the extraordinary encounter with Simeon, the "child's father and mother marveled" at what was said (Luke 2:33). Simeon then singles out Mary and forewarns her of "a sword that will pierce your own soul." She is then told by the prophetess Anna that her son would bring redemption to Jerusalem. This day at the temple must have astounded and humbled Mary and Joseph. How would they reconcile the blessing and burden of being Jesus' parents? What resources or sympathizers would they have, but each other?

God provided for Mary and Jesus when he sent the angel to Joseph. He would be Mary's protector, provider, lover, and the earthly father of Jesus. Remember the words of Matthew 1:25, "he took his wife, but knew her not until she had given birth to a son. And he called his name Jesus." Joseph does what a father does by naming the child. He does what a husband does by being physically intimate with his wife. It is an oft overlooked aspect of God's provision that Mary was given a husband in the truest sense of the word. This also means Jesus had a human family in the complete sense of the concept. Theirs is no bogus or sham family. And Jesus is no romanticized liberator.

In Mark 6:1-6 Jesus is rejected early in his ministry by those in his hometown of Nazareth. When they hear his preaching they are astonished at his brilliance. But instead of embracing Jesus, the people are offended that someone like them, a carpenter and son of Joseph and Mary, and brother of several siblings would show them up with such luminosity! Can you feel in your heart the sting Mary would have felt throughout Jesus' life every time someone made a reference to her hasty wedding? The profound level of misunderstanding Mary had to endure would be enough to disquiet any woman. Yet Mary lived humbly with the assumption on the part of others that Jesus was the product of sin!

As time went on and Jesus grew to the age of male accountability (i.e., the age of twelve), Mary and Joseph were thrown into a tizzy when Jesus declared his own independence at the temple. In Luke 2:40 he establishes that his life and occupation will not be what his elders expect, but about the business of his heavenly Father. In 2:51 we are told that Mary "treasured all these things in her heart." Throughout her lifetime, Mary's habit of treasuring and pondering would serve her well.

Praying To The Problem

The treasuring and pondering of Mary is also what separates us from the people of by-gone eras. We are busy doing and organizing our lives for success. We know more, do more, achieve more, travel farther, and live longer than any other generation. But do we live better? We are exposed to more experiences, but are we wiser? Are we even capable of meditating without the input of twenty close friends and experts? We should reserve more energy for prayer and meditation on God's word. By expressing our concerns to friends about matters that need prayer we might attain a false sense of having prayed when all that has really happened is talking to the problem. Let's first pray and encourage others to pray first and talk about the problem later. Spiritual power is harnessed when women join hands and "pray to the problem" together.

The Real Nativity
Once Joseph was in on the birth plans, he took complete responsibility for his bride. Whether or not they skipped the unnecessary formality (betrothal was legal and binding marriage) of the wedding ceremony, Joseph immediately takes Mary home with him and keeps her a virgin until the birth of Jesus. They journey to Bethlehem to register for the census and stay at least through Jesus' infancy. What was the hurry? Was it because Mary's pregnancy was controversial in her town of Nazareth? Were they taking advantage of the census as a legitimate excuse to leave town in the midst of gossip?

To the contemporary woman used to medical experts and sterilized surroundings, the manger scene of Christ's birth rouses pity on behalf of the young virgin mother. Yet, keep in mind the historical and cultural context. From girlhood Mary would have been taught by her mother and elders everything there was to know about childbirth. With less formal education than modern women, Mary would still have known and seen more about the birthing process than most of us today. Along with her confidence in Hebrew midwifery traditions, Mary had strong assurances from Gabriel that the baby would be fine.

Mary would need more than the usual amount of bravery required for bringing a child into the world. She would need to trust Joseph, a man with whom she probably hadn't spent much time alone. Since Matthew 1:25 makes it clear that Joseph did not have sexual relations with Mary until after the birth of Jesus, she was sexually inexperienced and a virgin during her labor with her first child. The birth of a first child is always a risk in terms of outcome in the best of circumstances. Despite Mary's possible knowledge of midwifery and assurances from an angel, she would have concerns and anxieties. She would at least be disappointed not to have a place in the inn. Perhaps the stable turned out to be a blessing for its fresh straw and isolation. However, the realist in me suspects that regardless of the surroundings, Mary was in a strange town and place, away from her mother, and probably challenged to see the beauty at the time.

By the time Mary has birthed Jesus she has overcome more than most women will ever encounter. She has been visited by an angel and told that she would miraculously conceive the long awaited Messiah. She has been encouraged and affirmed by her cousin Elizabeth who has a similar miracle to report. And Mary has had the daunting task of facing a man of integrity who on one hand cannot bear the thought of humiliating her, nor be aligned in marriage with a seemingly immoral woman. By the time they journey to Bethlehem, Mary has been faithful to God, vindicated by Joseph's encounter with the angel Gabriel, and is ready to take on any challenge with her man by her side.

There are subtle differences between what the Bible gives as the sequence of events (carefully putting together the accounts in Matthew and Luke) in this first Christmas and the romanticized versions of cards and movies. These differences are very revealing in regards to the Mary I've heard about and the authentic, flesh and blood Mary of Scripture.

The Magi
In Matthew we have the account of the visit of the Wise Men. After Jesus was born in Bethlehem wise men (magi in Greek) from the east came to Jerusalem asking for the whereabouts of the newly born king of the Jews. They had seen and followed his star and came to worship him. When Herod in Jerusalem heard this he was troubled, "and all Jerusalem with him." Herod took the claims of the magi seriously, they naively revealed their mission, and this caused Herod to assemble the chief priests and scribes to

ascertain all prophecies of the Christ. When Herod was displeased, all Jerusalem was too. The learned scholars had no trouble finding such prophecies. They brought to Herod's attention Micah 5:2: "And you, O Bethlehem, in the land of Judah, are by no means least among the rulers of Judah; for from you shall come a ruler who will shepherd my people Israel." The scribes and local citizens of Jerusalem knew Herod's lust for power. They knew he would not stand for any rivals, newborn or old. They must have known the implications of the magi's unapprised mission. When the magi were later summoned to meet with Herod in secret he told them where to go and to return with a report for him so that he could locate the child for the purpose of "worshipping" him.

Upon reaching Bethlehem the Magi followed the star which led them to the house in which Jesus and his family were then living. Matthew 2:11 tells us that they came into the house and "saw the child with Mary his mother, and they fell down and worshiped him." Then they offered him gifts of gold, frankincense and myrrh. They were sincerely seeking after God. They didn't understand the complexity of the situation they had walked into. In fact, the "wise men" were so naive that they had to be warned in a dream not to return to Herod. This dream must have occurred after they left, because Joseph also had to be warned in a dream to flee to Egypt.

Joseph then "rose and took the child and his mother by night and departed to Egypt and remained there until the death of Herod. This was to fulfill what the Lord had spoken by the prophet, 'Out of Egypt I called my son.'" Matthew knew this would be significant for his Jewish readers when he authored this gospel. Mary's son would be worshiped at her breast for his divine presence. The history of the world would revolve around the birth and ministry of her son.

Flight to Egypt
The faith of Mary and Joseph would have been greatly bolstered and challenged after this episode. They would have needed a dream

to convince them to leave their comfortable haven in Bethlehem. Otherwise they would never have had a reason to suspect danger was coming in the form of "Herod's guard sent to kill all the male children in Bethlehem and all that region under two years of age." This was also the fulfillment of a tragic prophecy: "A voice was heard in Ramah, weeping and loud lamentation, Rachel weeping for her children; she refused to be comforted, because they are no more." (Jer. 31:15) The literal reference is to the weeping of mothers over the exiles taken in the Babylonian captivity. The fuller meaning of Matthew's reference is that Israel will once again be oppressed in the slaughter of "innocent babes" by an evil ruler. Rumors of this atrocity would have reached Joseph and Mary. They would have carried sorrow in their hearts for the victims left behind. They would have been humbled that their Son was spared, and horrified that he was the cause.

Under Joseph's leadership, Mary and her little family would flee to the land of Egypt. She would leave all that was familiar and lose the opportunity to see Elizabeth. Jesus and John would not be raised together as she might have hoped. Would the family of Joseph find refuge and anonymity in the bustling city of Alexandria, Egypt which had a larger Jewish population than Jerusalem? It is believed that the precious gifts from the magi would have been more than sufficient to support the family.

They returned after Herod died, but not to the village of Joseph. One of Herod's most evil sons was ruling in that region, forcing Joseph to take his family to the city of Nazareth, Mary's hometown. Another prophecy would be fulfilled: "He shall be called a Nazarene." She would have to live among family and neighbors who knew her story. Mary would certainly have been surrounded by critics and doubters who knew her claims of angels and virgin births. Imagine the vastness of being the mother of the One for whom prophets spoke and the universe revolves. The tip of the sword was already poised upon Mary's heart.

Collision With Convention

Let's turn our attention to the eventual start of Jesus' public ministry and its collision with conventional thought. From reading the Gospel of John (not to mention all four of the gospels) one gets the idea that the most religiously informed of Jesus' day were quite confused about the nature, role, and mission of the Messiah. The very religious Jews, especially the Pharisees, knew references from their scriptures which foretold his eventual advent, but their perspective was stunted by pride. This mode of general knowledge about a coming Messiah combined with an aloof response to His message is so prevalent among the religious elite that I believe it warrants a name: truth challenged: a state of knowing the truth without being appropriately affected by it!

In John 1 there is a persistent, in-your-face cry of truth from John the Baptist, Elizabeth and Zechariah's son. His call to repentance is in preparation for the coming Messiah, a messiah with whom John has no personal acquaintance (Jn. 1:33). After John baptizes Jesus, Jesus is driven by the Holy Spirit into the wilderness for forty days of fasting and temptation. His sinless and divine nature is upheld by his Scripture saturated resistance to the devil (cf. Matthew 4; Mark 1; and Luke 4). He then attends a wedding in Cana in Galilee, along with his mother and his disciples.

Something happens which propels Jesus into the spot light at the wedding—His mom makes a request! The wine has run out and Mary knows Jesus can fix the problem for the hosts. If any human knows his abilities and potential it's Mary. Perhaps since his baptism she has been looking for the right opportunity to showcase his abilities. Possibly Mary wants Jesus to let everyone there know that he is more than just a prophet or leader. It is clear from John that Mary has an agenda to promote Jesus. This is not a bad thing, but surely we will see hints of her flawed wisdom. Jesus takes a jab at what may have been her conventional understanding of Messiah. But he honors his mother because he is loving and flexible.

I'm not sure how big of a social blunder it was to run out of wine in first century Israel. The situation may have presented a dilemma unique to their time and culture. Perhaps having thirteen additional men (not including some of their families) dried up the bar! Whatever the case, Mary saw fit to bring Jesus into it.

God used Mary to set the stage for Jesus' first public miracle. And don't be surprised by the hints of a difference between her motives and Jesus' ultimate motive!

I prefer to avoid analyzing the symbolic nature of this miracle. Others have done better justice to it than I could. In our study of Mary we must notice the intriguing nature of Mary's involvement.

Here is the dialogue between mother and son:

> "When the wine was gone, Jesus' mother said to him, 'They have no more wine.'
> 'Dear woman, why do you involve me?' Jesus replied, 'My time has not yet come.'
> His mother said to the servants, 'Do whatever he tells you.'"
>
> *John 2:3*

Jesus basically tells his mom "This isn't my problem." Evidently Mary isn't influenced by Jesus' lack of concern. She tells the servants, "Do whatever he tells you." Jesus then gives orders to the servants to fill the six stone water jars with water. In verse 8 they are told to draw some out and take it to "the master of the banquet". When the master of the banquet tastes the wine, not knowing where it comes from, he says to the bridegroom, "Everyone brings out the choice wine first and then the cheaper wine after the guests have had too much to drink; but you have saved the best till now." This first of Jesus' signs reveals his glory and honors his host (John 2:11).

One possibility here is that Mary just wanted Jesus to seize the opportunity to debut his supernatural talent. Perhaps preparations for the back up wine were feasible for the host. Whatever the case, it is Jesus' response that says it all. Here we turn our attention to

Jesus' collision with his mother's conventional thought.

Jesus' response gives us a hint about Mary's view of his messianic ministry. Certainly she believes in and supports him, but she is, like all of us, a product of her times. Throughout Jesus' ministry his followers and enemies alike misunderstand his mission. Of course Mary, like others, was anxious for Jesus to roll up his sleeves and get to work on saving Israel. It is only natural that she would not be able to comprehend the methodical workings of her son's mission. In the many references Jesus made to "my time" he was referring to the time of his arrest and crucifixion. His disciples who loved him and wanted him to succeed were slow to get this! His "time" wasn't really understood by his followers as literal death and sacrifice. Jesus already knew that redemption for his people would be purchased by his own blood. Not by miracles. The miracles would reveal His glory, but lead to something unthinkable—crucifixion. Jesus knew that his "time" would come only after following the will of the Father, a carefully crafted and divine scheme.

But Jesus' mom is used to being honored and respected by her children. She directs the servants to listen to Jesus. She may not understand everything Jesus does, but she knows his power. Most likely she wants to use that to bless the wedding couple. For this would be the best wine ever served!

Yes, Jesus is working on the divine time table, but he's also flexible. He honors his mother, the party hosts, and most of all reveals his glory. As a result of this his disciples believe in him.

Sharing Her Son With the World
Mary simply wants to share her son with the world. We must admire her for this, because every time Jesus gave to others she and the rest of their family would be deprived of his attention. In human form, the Son of God was limited by time and space. But Mary believed in Jesus so much that she was willing to make personal sacrifices and suffer personal slights to share her son, God's Son, with the world. How our mothering would be

improved if we knew that we are called to share our children and that by sending them out others would be brought to God. May we today be as prepared and eager as Mary was to share the fruit of our labor with the world in need of a savior.

The quality of my mothering is greatly raised when I remember the passion Mary had for Jesus and his ministry. She knew she gave birth to him for this purpose: to become the Messiah of his people. He was given to her by God so that she and Joseph could raise him in a loving, godly home until the time for him to be sent into the world. Notice from John 1:3 that Jesus was sent and given authority by God's Holy Spirit, not Mary or any other human. His authority, mission, and ability all came from God. Mary was a humble, loving, generous, and visionary mother. But even Mary would have to witness the unfolding of God's plan for the Messiah.

A Sword Will Pierce Your Own Soul

Mary, Jesus' brothers, and his disciples accompanied Jesus to Capernaum. Scholars agree that Joseph may have been deceased by this time. It seems that Jesus was very close to his family and did spend time with them even after the start of his ministry, which suggests a couple of things about Jesus as a man.

The first thing to notice is that the Capernaum retreat is right after Jesus has revealed his glory in Cana. His disciples believe in him. Yet, Jesus chooses to focus on relationships and not "ministry plans." Actually, from the wedding on, the disciples seem to be adopted into Jesus' immediate family. This must have been largely due to Mary's generous and loving spirit. He was not just her son; He's the Son of Man!

The second thing John 2:12-23 makes clear is that Jesus is full of purpose and integrity. When he goes to Jerusalem his aim is to speak and live the truth. He will free people from the lies of the corrupt leaders. The gentle, loving son of Mary is also the Son of God. The Jesus who indulges his mother at the wedding and spends a few days bonding is also not shy of making enemies.

There are things worth fighting for.

Jesus, who lived his whole earthly life to do the will of the Father, knew what was worth fighting for, and it wasn't his career! It was and is the glory of God. The corrupt temple authorities allowed the temple to become a market place instead of a house of worship. When Jesus made a whip out of cords and marched into the temple (2:15), he was ready to draw blood. Ironically, in terms of rabbinical success, this was suicide.

It is my speculation that when Mary heard about Jesus' temple confrontation she must have been uniquely impacted by it. When his ministry was getting off to such a beautiful start, why did her son have to pit himself against the very people whose favor he should be courting? This would be such a difficult thing for any mother to understand. Scripture indicates in Mark 3:31 that Jesus had brothers who did not receive any special treatment from him while he ministered. For any brother or family member to possibly resent frequent run-ins with religious leaders would be reasonable. The misconceptions about Jesus' methods and the resulting emotional and family conflicts may well have been the sword that would pierce Mary's heart (Luke 2:35). For three years this woman would see her son exalted, followed, maligned, misunderstood, and betrayed by his own people. A far cry from the often romanticized ideal the early first century Jews had of Messiah.

Ordinary Saint

In Luke 11:27 we have an intriguing reference to a woman in a crowd who called out a blessing to Jesus while he was preaching and casting out demons. She raised her voice and said to Jesus, "Blessed is the womb that bore you, and the breasts at which you nursed!" Caught up in the excitement of Jesus' power over demons, and filled with love, this woman could not contain her emotion. Her emotions and heart intentions were right. Jesus didn't deny his mother's significance. But he did rebuke the woman with, "Blessed rather are those who hear the word of God and keep it!" He doesn't ignore her or treat her like a heckler. Jesus lovingly teaches her a wider spiritual truth: All who love God and obey him are blessed! One doesn't have to be related to Jesus by blood to belong to him. One doesn't need to be among the elite Pharisees or other religious leaders to be important to God. He blesses all who come to him in faith and obedience!

In the face of such gracious godliness it is easy to idolize Mary in much the same way as the enthusiastic woman in the crowd. We don't have any biblical record of Mary's sins, nor do we have biblical reason to forget her humanity. She was a wife, mother, and fellow sinner. She was indeed blessed among women, but not to the exclusion of sin and suffering. Jesus' mother knew the hurt of stigma early in life. Mary also must have known the usual pains and joys of motherhood since we believe she bore children subsequent to the birth of Jesus. In Mark 3:20 we are clued in to the challenge it must have been to be part of Jesus' immediate family.

We are told there that Jesus' family tried to "take charge of him," for they believed he had "gone out of his mind." From a human standpoint this family concern seems legitimate. After all, Jesus isn't exactly following the prescribed course for rabbinical success. He's offending leaders in every camp and amassing a crowd of riff-raff followers. Possibly Mary is concerned about Jesus' mental stability. It is also plausible that his mother was merely accompanying her family in an attempt to be a stabilizing force. She may simply have feared that he would be engulfed by the pressing crowds that gathered, "so that he and his disciples were not even able to eat."

How does a mother know when to nurture and when to stay away and let her child suffer? Mary, of all women, must have been incredibly nurturing! How could she not want to follow her son everywhere and drag along the family to keep tabs on him? Doesn't every good mother adore her baby when he's born and vows to protect him with her life? Maybe Mary had advice for Jesus. Perhaps she had a warning about his need for a healthier schedule. Or certainly she just loved him and wanted him to still be part of the family unit. But Jesus wasn't just her son. He was the Son of God. When he was born she had to share him. Now in the thick of ministry she had to share him.

Near The Cross
In the midst of torturous execution Mary stood near the cross of Jesus. John 19:25 makes a point of Mary's close proximity to the cross and posture which suggests she is not in a sobbing heap or hysterics at the height of her son's agony. She takes her place with loyal dignity and quietly receives comfort from Jesus himself. Even in the throes of death, Our Lord demonstrates compassion for Mary and others. He tells John, who is with her, to be as a son to Mary and vice versa.

Could it be that as the sword took its final plunge into Mary's heart, she serenely understood the ultimate mission of her Son? At the cross was Mary comforted by the sense that the scene before her was planned by the Heavenly Father of her Son? Who among us women can help but feel admiration and reverence for the woman who stood weeping, but did not crumble; who needed to be comforted, but did not recoil from her own suffering?

It is in the gospel of John that we have the only account of Mary, mother of Jesus, at the cross. It is also in this same account that we see something to which Mary would have been privy: the Roman soldiers casting lots for her son's garment. Even at his death, Mary would have to share her son with the world.

We read in John 19:23 that they "took his clothes, dividing them into four shares, one for each of them, with the undergarment remaining. This garment was seamless, woven in one piece from top to bottom. 'Let's not tear it,' they said to one another. 'Let's decide by lot who will get it.' This happened that the Scripture might be fulfilled which said, 'They divided my garments among them and cast lots for my clothing.'"

Many assume that the casting of lots was customary for all crucifixions. Now that I realize it was Jesus' undergarment left remaining which the soldiers wanted, I think differently about this casting of lots. This may be best explained in present tense as if we are standing at the scene of the crucifixion:

Picture the harsh and resolute Roman soldiers ordering the placing of the beams of wood onto the ground at the site of execution. The large beams are secured to the rope that will raise the crosses. They then begin to forcibly lower each convicted man (three that day) onto his cross. There usually ensues great struggle and resistance on the part of the convict who has nothing to loose at this point. On this day two men in particular are vehement while one remains quiet. Add to this the mounting pressure on the soldiers from the growing crowd of mostly followers and some mockers of the one prisoner called Jesus of Nazareth.

As a perk of their trade the soldiers are entitled to hastily strip the clothing from each prisoner to sell or use the possessions of the doomed convicts. They customarily prefer their wards naked to further punish and degrade them for their crimes. But they stop when they see the undergarment on Jesus. The soldiers can spot high quality, seamless fabric when they see it, and they all covet it. And imagine such a find on a common criminal! So they agree not to tear it or rip it off his body. When he is dead and removed from the cross the one who casts the lucky lot would win the prize. This speculative train of thought is plausible if the soldiers removed Jesus' garment earlier for his scourging and put it back on him along with the purple robe mentioned in John 19:2.

Perhaps Mary, John, and all the other followers of Jesus present were relieved to see their Lord with some remaining covering. One wonders if the Roman guards maintained much interest in the garment by the end of the ordeal. The words of Jesus, the disappearance of the sun, and the earth tremors might have put a few things in perspective for them. The undergarment of Jesus was spared, but the veil in the temple was torn and the Roman centurion in Luke 23:47 declared, "Surely, this was a righteous man." I don't believe the remaining garment of Jesus was of importance to the Romans at the end.

One might ask: "As a single, itinerant preacher, from whom could Jesus accept such an intimate and valuable gift?" Possibly this highly coveted garment was lovingly woven and made for Jesus by his mother. If so, what satisfaction would Mary later find in knowing that her gift to Jesus was used to fulfill prophecy! Apart from the quality of the undergarment, there would have been no reason for the soldiers to have left it remaining as a prize! These details are significant because they demonstrate the way God orchestrates human events for his own purposes. Mary saw prophecy fulfilled utterly and completely regarding her son's sacrificial death.

Surprising Strength
Mary's personal journey from the stable to the cross is especially unique and challenging to women. It tells us that God values the part a mother plays in the details of her child's life—even in the life of the Son of God. Mary inspires us to believe in a God of miracles in the midst of a broken world. Mary inspires us to treasure and love the glory of God, even at great personal sacrifice. Her humility was the window through which God showed her his glorious promises.

Mary would have continued to mother the siblings of Jesus. She would have been a mother to John and perhaps he a comfort to her in the absence of faith on the part of her other children. She must have silently known that Jesus would not remain in the grave. When Jesus rose from the dead on the third day, Mary would have recognized him instantly. She wouldn't have begrudged the others who saw him first. She was used to sharing him! Mary Magdalene and the other women who kept close to Mary were not afraid to go to the tomb or carry on with their women's work. Perhaps Mary's certainty in her Son influenced them. I imagine her taking hold of her risen son and searching for the wound in his side. I envisage Mary telling loved ones of the fulfilled prophecies which revolved around Jesus. Mary was likely a great and nurturing encouragement to the Apostles in Jerusalem when she prayed and waited for the Holy Spirit with them in Acts 1:14.

Then and now Mary remains in our hearts the greatest mother of all: The mother of God's Son; the humble, joyful, thankful, and brave woman who lived her life as other women, yet with a sword gradually piercing her generous heart. From now on all generations will call her blessed.

Two millennia later we have through Mary a challenge: The lives of all women who are full of faith, however humble, can partake of the glory of God. The glory of God is seen when we mother and nurture and hope and suffer and pray and worship and cling to the promises of The Holy One of Israel. Mary's passion for the glory of God brings true confidence and strength which cannot be shaken by the ravages of time. May we be able to count ourselves blessed in our own generation. May our children be raised with the same passion Mary had; to nurture the flame of Christ within each child who will someday take that light out into the world.

Questions for Study and Discussion:

1. In reading Luke 1 and 2, what do Mary's responses to the angel and her situation reveal about her heart and character? Site specific examples from scripture.

2. How do you perceive Joseph's role?

3. If the only thing you knew about Mary were from "The Magnificat" (Luke 1:46-55), how would you characterize her faith? How does your worship characterize you?

4. Mary hurried to see her older cousin Elizabeth as soon as she was visited by Gabriel. What do you see that the two women might have given each other during this time?

5. Re-read John 2:4 and 19:6. What do you think might have been some of Mary's struggles concerning Jesus? How did her son treat her in these two references?

6. What about Mary's life challenges you personally?

7. If you were Mary, listening to Jesus' critics, how would you defend him?

8. What do you believe is significant about Mary standing at the foot of the cross?

9. In John 2:3 Jesus tells his mother that his time has not come. The same phrase is used in Matthew 6:18; Mark. 14:35; and John 8:20. Based on these verses and all that the gospels tell of Jesus' earthly ministry, what is meant by "my time"?

10. What parallels do you see between prophecy given in Isaiah 53 and Jesus' life, death, and resurrection?

3

SARAH: CHERISHED PRINCESS

Scripture References:
Genesis 12-23 • Hebrews 11:8-12
Galatians 4:21-31 • 1 Peter 3:1-7

"Let your adorning be the hidden person of the heart with the imperishable beauty of a gentle and quiet spirit...For this is how the holy women who hoped in God used to adorn themselves, by submitting to their husbands, as Sarah obeyed Abraham, calling him lord. And you are her children, if you do well and do not fear anything that is frightening." (1 Peter 3:5)

Sarah is cited by the Apostle Peter as a model of holy submission for Christian wives. Sarah, like the other matriarchs, was a woman whose entire life revolved around the call her husband received from God. His call was her call. There were major challenges about their lives which were characterized by crisis and required extraordinary faith. To our generation Sarah's support and devotion to her husband seem like a phenomenon. To the holy women of the past this was just a thing called marriage. Is she mentioned by Peter as a sort of history lesson? I think we will find that Sarah has much more to teach her "daughters" who live millennia and cultures apart from her ancient wisdom.

Secondly, Sarah's style of submission is complex and does not fit the modern stereotype of doormat women to which some wives descend. Her personality contains an edge of wit and determination. Abraham's call would have been a challenge for even the most compliant of wives. Though submissive, Sarah was not without personal views, ambitions, or passions. Yet, the challenges and frustrations of their lifelong call helped create a gutsy resilience in Sarah's personality. Sarah's story is about marriage in a world of conflict and frustrated goals. Like all of our lives, her story was just a part of God's bigger glory. Her submission was not perfect, neither was her husband's leadership. But their enduring romance, not a sentimental one, provides inspiration and challenge for women of today who need an example of holy femininity.

Beautiful and Holy
What does it look like to be a holy woman? At the end of this study we will have a vivid portrayal of holy beauty from the life of Sarah. The world we live in does not place a high premium on holiness. Certainly, secular culture does not associate holiness with beauty, except perhaps of an ethereal and weak sort. Religious groups and churches often link holiness with a disdain for physical beauty, as if the two are incongruent. It is undeniable that Sarah is considered by Moses (the author of Genesis) and Peter to be physically beautiful. Interestingly, the biblical authors do not consider the details to be as important as the mere perception of her beauty.

In the context of Scripture, Sarah's beauty is extremely important to the story of Abraham's life call. According to the accounts of Genesis 12 through 20 Sarah was so physically beautiful that on at least two occasions she was taken from her husband by rulers who coveted her for themselves. She was so beautiful that her husband had to plan for ways to protect and keep her. She was seen as her husband's most valued asset! Ironically, Peter cites as Sarah's most desirable feature, her "imperishable beauty of a gentle and quiet spirit, which in God's eyes is very precious." This passage of Peter's is so packed with meaning and application for us today that we will return to it throughout this study.

Understanding Sarah requires familiarity with her husband

and their world. If you will pour over Scripture with me, we can identify with Sarai and her family even though they are worlds apart from us!

Step with me into the world of Sarai, later known as Sarah, which means "princess." You live in a world of pagan customs, beliefs, and practices. The peoples of your society have been corrupted by pagan ways and tainted by the "Nephilim" of Genesis 6:2. After the flood of Noah the second irruption of these progeny of fallen angels had infected the land of Canaan (Gen. 12:6). Presumably your family has sought to protect against the commingling by practicing a modicum of inbreeding. You are married to your father's son, Abram, by another marriage. Your uncle Nabor is married to his deceased brother's daughter. Leaving behind Nabor, your father; Terah, with his son; Abram, grandson Lot, and you, his daughter/daughter-in-law, go forth together from Ur of the Chaldeans into the land of Canaan. But something happens to keep your family from reaching the destination of Canaan. Instead, they settle in Haran where Terah, the man with the vision to leave his homeland, eventually dies at the age of two hundred and five.

The Call Affirmed

> Gen. 12:1-3 "Now the Lord said [had said] to Abram, 'Go from your country and your kindred and your father's house to the land that I will show you. And I will make of you a great nation, and I will bless you and make your name great, so that you will be a blessing. I will bless those who bless you, and him who dishonors you I will curse, and in you all the families of the earth will be blessed.' (ESV)

Even before Genesis 12, there was a vision for the place called Canaan. This dream was likely driven in part by the need to escape the idol worship and wickedness found in the cultures of Terah's homeland, as well as to avoid the presence of the nephilim (first mentioned in Gen. 6:1-4) who were known as giants of renown super human strength. For whatever reason, the goal of Canaan seems to have been dormant for some time while the family settled in Haran. Perhaps the family was afraid to venture into the frightening place. And then one day, after his father's death, Abram hears God calling him back to his destiny! Genesis 12:1 refers to the fact that God had called Abram. The "said" in 12:1 is literally translated "had said."

It is unsure whether or not Terah knew God or even had spiritual reasons for leaving his homeland. We do know from Acts 7:2-4 that the call of God was specifically directed to Abram as quoted by Stephen: "The God of glory appeared to our father Abraham when he was living in Mesopotamia, before he was living in Haran...." So the strong implication is that Abram had a special relationship with God early on which motivated him to leave his home land twice. Joshua 24:2 confirms the pagan background of Terah. Yet, Genesis 11:31 suggests that Terah was the earthly initiator, "Terah took Abram his son and Lot the son of Haran, his grandson, and Sarai...and they went forth together from Ur...." One recurring theme of Scripture is that not all who play a part understand their role, but God orchestrates everything with perfect timing!

When Abram and his family reach Canaan (12:6-7) they pass through the land to the oft referred to oak tree of Moreh in Shechem. According to Genesis 12:6b "at that time the Canaanites were in the land," which is likely a reference to the offspring of the fallen angels, nephilim, who irrupted throughout history to thwart God's plan of redemption for man. Abraham's out of the way route seems to have been due to the threatening presence of the Canaanites, which included the very intimidating nephilim who had commingled among the peoples and nations of Canaan. There in Shechem, for the first time recorded, the Lord appeared to Abram and gave the promise, "To your offspring I will give this land." In response Abram builds an altar to the Lord. From there Abram moves to the hill country east of Bethel (Gen.

12:8), pitches his tent, and builds another altar to the Lord, and does something completely appropriate yet revolutionary: he calls upon the name of the Lord.

Abram the Sojourner
Before addressing the controversial events in Egypt, let's take notice of something very characteristic of Abram. He worships God. Whenever God appears to Abram throughout these passages, Abram's response is to worship. But he doesn't worship a distant, unknown God. He worships his God by name! God introduces Himself to Abram by name: Yahweh. In other words, Abram has a personal faith.

Can you imagine the desperate need Abram must have felt for God, especially after leaving his homeland to follow the call. Can you believe the faith it would take to be certain that God would come through on these staggering promises? Is it not remarkable that in the presence of hostile, dominant peoples and strange beings, Abraham would have the faith to be the only man to follow the call of God? I am struck by Abram's total dependency on God. From the beginning, God reveals his presence to Abram so that he will know that his God is glorious and worthy of worship. Abram is willing to take incredible risks for the God he calls by name. Setting up altars to worship God is a pattern of devotion for Abram. If sincere worship is any indication of one's true motives, Abram's conscience is presented by Scripture as clear.

Considering Abram's obedience and faith, and the lack of textual indicators to the contrary, Abram's decision to sojourn in Egypt during a time of famine may be seen as a sound, though risky decision. This necessity of constant traveling and sojourning leads to another reality for Abram. Wherever he pitches his tent in the neighboring lands of Canaan (which he cannot yet possess), he is at high risk of facing hostile forces. At every border, rulers and war lords (including some nephilim) may search his possessions and demand payment of some kind. At every turn of his sojourning he will have to explain himself or be willing to fight a bloody battle. Should he deplete his resources and become preoccupied with battle tactics to protect his own life and his family? Many have criticized (though scripture itself does not!) Abram for his approach to this dilemma and fail to see the big picture of what God is doing throughout the book of Genesis.

Abram: The Point Man
When Abram is about to enter Egypt in Gen 12:11 he lays out to Sarai what I believe to be their survival strategy for the course of their sojourn in and around the Promised Land. He says to Sarai, "I know that you are a woman beautiful in appearance, and when the Egyptians see you, they will say, 'This is his wife.' Then they will kill me, but they will let you live. Say you are my sister, that it may go well with me because of you, and that my life may be spared for your sake." In Abram's defense, it would hardly be beneficial for Sarai if her husband dies in a battle over her. How could it be anything but equally beneficial for Sarai and Abram to help each other avoid rape and murder?! This reasoning of Abram's is unjustly maligned by some who from a modern perspective see his leadership here as flawed. I will attempt to show from Scripture that the opposite is true. Abram the leader comes up with a plan to preserve his family—an effective plan, which the Bible itself does not criticize.

At this point, Genesis 12:5 indicates that Abram is fairly well off, with livestock, possessions, and servants when he comes to Canaan. Theses people and possessions are likely the accumulations of a shrewd businessman. His greatest asset must be Sarai. Sure enough, when they entered Egypt, the princes of Pharaoh reported her beauty to Pharaoh, she was sent for and taken. Apart from the big picture this may seem like bad news. For Abram and Sarai this will be a definite challenge. Stay with me on this to see how Abram's strategy will be a vehicle for the glory of God.

Remember when we observed that Abram called on the name of the Lord? I believe that God's desire to bring fame to his name is the crux of the whole matter here. This account is not about Abram's and Sarai's deception. It's about what God is doing behind the scenes to make His name known among the nations!

First, let's examine Abram's possible choices in this matter. I suppose he could deface his wife's beauty or make her "dress down." But that might be rather cowardly of him and humiliating for her. Another idea would be to arm his men and tell them to be prepared for battle. Even if he wins he would have to repeat this scenario every time he enters a new land or encounters another interested "suitor." At this point there is no reason to doubt Abram's bravery and valor in battle, which will be demonstrated later when he rescues Lot. No one can accuse the man of cowardice! Neither is Abram's sojourning supposed to be about fighting off his wife's admirers.

Culturally, there is one solution which just might also be an opportunity to save lives and make a statement. In ancient times (and until recent history) the only way a man could have another man's wife is by making her a widow. But if she is single it is expected that suitors (no matter their station in life) must strike a deal for her hand in marriage. Sarah's barrenness would make it easier to pass her off as a sister instead of his wife. Here we see the seeds of Abram's great talent for negotiating. He's patient and he knows that God will protect him and Sarai. He knows something about his God. So, in Genesis 12:11-13, Abram lays out their survival strategy. He says to his wife, "Say you are my sister...." This is not for selfish gain or evil purposes. It is simply what I believe he needed to do whenever they entered a foreign land. Sarai trusts, submits, and does not fear this frightening thing her husband asks of her. And they wait for God to reveal himself to Pharaoh and everyone else!

The Frightening Thing: Say You Are My Sister

> When Abram entered Egypt, the Egyptians saw that the woman was very beautiful. And when the princes of Pharaoh

saw her, they praised her to Pharaoh. And the woman was taken into Pharaoh's house. And for her sake he dealt well with Abram; and he had sheep, oxen, male donkeys, male servants, female servants, female donkeys, and camels.

Genesis 12:14-16 (ESV)

Sarai must have been remarkable to have attracted so much attention! Whatever natural dyes and ointments made from berries and herbs available back then couldn't have been much help if one wasn't naturally attractive. Given the limitations of ancient beauty treatments, it is hopefully not too speculative to assume that there were not very many women in their sixties still possessing all their teeth, hair, fine boned beauty, and feminine poise. Instead of being a faded beauty, Sarai is a cherished princess. Much credit for this should be given to Abram for being a godly husband. Women flourish under the love and affirmation of a strong leader.

During the time Sarai was taken into the household of Pharaoh, she would have gone through the period of purification customarily required by ancient rulers. It was during this time that Sarai is protected from contact with Pharaoh, yet living in his household. It is also during this time that Pharaoh, her suitor, must pay his respects to Abram by lavishing him with impressive gifts. This shouldn't be too hard, right? After all, Pharoah must see Abram as a mere vagabond from nowhere fleeing a famine! So Pharaoh sends over a generous gift of livestock and servants.

Notice between Genesis 12:16-17 there is no action given on Abram's part. No displays of gratitude from Abram. No indications of any rejection either. Neither does he make any move to leave, which would be expected if he were satisfied with Pharaoh's wooing of Sarai. It appears that Abram was waiting on God. And God speaks in the form of grave sickness.

According to Genesis 12:17, "But the Lord afflicted Pharaoh and his house with great plagues because of Sarai, Abram's wife. So Pharaoh called Abram and said, "What is this you have done to me? Why did you not tell me that she was your wife? Why did you say, 'She is my sister,' so that I took her for my wife? Now then, here is your wife; take her, and go.' And Pharaoh gave men orders concerning him, and they sent him away with his wife and all that he had."

Here is where Scripture spells out its "number one" theme: God gets man's attention by unusual means in order to display his power and glory. At this point in our study, it may be tempting to rely on the microscope and focus on the details and insert one's own opinion about Abram the husband. Pick up the telescope for its wider view. What we see scripture focusing on is not the "lie of necessity" told by Abram, but the need for Pharaoh to understand more about Abram and his God. Pharaoh is now clued in to the fact that Sarai is Abram's wife. He never mentions "God" in verses 17-20, but Pharaoh seems to be aware of a supernatural power associated with Abram. Was this learned from Sarai, or Pharaoh's princes who might have kept a watch on Abram and his activities? Did Abram perhaps develop a reputation for worshipping a mysterious God?

Humbled by the plagues visited upon his household and the subsequent revelation of Sarai's true relationship with Abram, pharaoh hastily summons Abram. He claims ignorance and innocence, which we know was in the least preceded by sinful lust and covetousness! He blames Abram, and seems to be afraid of Abram. Weakened by sickness, he does not punish Abram. Pharaoh simply gives orders to his men to send them packing, and lets Abram and family leave with all their new possessions! The text implies that a profound impression has been made on Pharaoh and his people: Don't mess with Abram or his powerful God!

The problem with the big picture is one has to be open to self-denial. One might discover from the bird's eye view that one's own role is not a matter of urgency to God. If I were Sarai, I might be wondering at this point, how any of this sojourning life and dodging of lustful rulers could be conducive to bearing children with Abram. The big picture is sometimes hard on women.

Calling Upon the Name

Gen. 13:1-8 describes the prosperity of Abram and his family upon leaving Egypt and journeying into the Negeb. They journey on from the Negeb (vvs. 3-4) eventually back to the place between Bethel and Ai "to the place where Abram had made an altar at the first." Notice the revolutionary thing Abram repeats: "And there Abram called upon the name of the Lord." The right mix of intimacy with and reverence for God is uniquely demonstrated by Abram. The mystery surrounding Abram, his God, and the impact of their reputation on those he knew suggests that Abram reserved the name of God primarily for worship. Perhaps he did not sling it around in every encounter with every pagan he met. It was perhaps known that he called on his God by name, but I question whether Abram spoke freely about God by the name, Yahweh.

Marriage to a Generous Man

Abram's nephew Lot shares in the wealth because of his uncle's generosity. They are so rich in livestock that the land can't hold them. Whether the riches from Pharaoh were bequeathed to the men individually, or Abram was extremely generous in the cut he gave to Lot, both men's herdsmen are fighting over boundaries and livestock.

Abram sees the problem in Genesis 13:8-11 and proposes a solution to Lot. They need more space to accommodate their possessions and families (servants are part of the family in their culture), so Abram, the elder and leader makes an extremely magnanimous offer to his younger nephew. He could have negotiated in a way that put Lot at a disadvantage, but instead he allows Lot to survey the land and choose for himself where to settle his own family. Genesis 13:11 says "Lot chose for himself all the Jordan Valley and moved his tent as far as Sodom. Now the men of Sodom were wicked great sinners against the Lord."

It might be pleasant to be associated with such a generous leader. On the other hand, it might also have been a challenge for Sarai.

Now she looses the companionship of Lot's wife and daughters, and the prime location for real estate, cultural opportunities, and shopping. Sodom was a very happening place of great worldly advantages. It must have attracted Lot for a reason! This is entirely speculative, but Sarai might have struggled with this change. She would certainly be more isolated and friendless. But she would see in the long run that her husband's generosity towards Lot proved to be her family's survival.

Maybe at this particular time Abram needed some encouragement. In Genesis 13:14 God said to Abram after Lot had separated from him, "Lift up your eyes and look from the place where you are, northward and southward and eastward and westward, for all the land that you see I will give to you and to your offspring as the dust of the earth, so that if one count the dust of the earth, your offspring also can be counted. Arise, walk through the length and the breadth of the land, for I will give it to you." Talk about receiving affirmation! So Abram moved his tent, settled by the oaks of Mamre in Hebron and "there he built an altar to the Lord." It seems that faith, obedience, and remembering God's promises make for excellent worship!

Marriage to a Valiant Defender
Genesis 14:1-11 gives the historical and technical background of a lengthy war between the King of Sodom and his 4 allies against 4 other nations. It might interest some to analyze the events, but for our purposes we will cut to the chase!! Sodom was invaded, plundered, and robbed by its enemies who also kidnapped Lot and all his possessions (v.12).

An escapee informed Abram and two of his allies, Eshcol and Aner, of the captivity of Lot. In the words of 14:14 "When Abram heard that his kinsman had been taken captive, he led forth his trained men, born in his house, three hundred and eighteen of them, and went in pursuit as far as Dan. And he divided his forces against them by night, he and his servants, and defeated them and pursued them to Hobah, north of Damascus. Then he brought back all the possessions and also brought back his kinsman Lot with his possessions, and the women and the people." The people referred to are the citizens taken from Sodom. Let it be noted that Abram is not afraid to fight for or defend his family. When necessity demanded it, Abram was valiant in his rescue of Lot. As we are about to see, Abram is also not motivated by greed or vanity.

In Genesis 14:17-24 we get a priceless glimpse into the character of Abram. After winning the war, the king of Sodom (notice that Abram is never listed as one of his allies!) goes out to meet Abram and confer the terms of release for the return of the Sodomites which Abram rescued. From the account of these verses it seems that the king of Sodom was present when Abram is also meeting with Melchizedek king of Salem. As priest of God Most High, Melchizedek declares, "Blessed be Abram by God Most High, Possessor of heaven and earth; and blessed be God Most High, who has delivered your enemies into your hand!"

Abram's response was to tithe a tenth of everything he owned to the priest. This was a remarkable act of faith for Abram, but probably misunderstood by the pagan king of Sodom. If the king of Sodom thought this tithe would make Abram vulnerable to greed he was wrong. Neither was Abram flattered by the attention. In what was probably an effort to secure the valiant Abram as an indebted vassal, the king offers to let Abram keep all the goods for himself if he will agree to hand over the recaptured people. Abram's answer is stunning in contrast to the greed and opportunism expected of him: "I have lifted my hand to the Lord, God Most High, Possessor of heaven and earth, that I would not take a thread or a sandal strap or anything that is yours, lest you should say, 'I have made Abram rich.' I will take nothing but what the young men have eaten, and the share of the men who went with me. Let Aner, Eshcol, and Mamre take their share." Abram could have negotiated for his own material good. Instead he openly refers to Yahweh and declares his allegiance to God Most High.

The Covenant Unfolds
Just when Abram has declined the offer of vast riches and alienated himself from a ruler, the word of the Lord comes to him, wades him in the night, and says in a vision: "Fear not, Abram, I am your shield; your reward shall be very great." Abram asks in 15:2, "What will you give me, for I continue childless, and the heir of my house is Eliezer of Damascus?" Then the Lord assures Abram that Eliezer will not be his heir, but that he will have a son from his own loins. Not only that, but Abram's descendants will number as the stars in heaven. The distressed Abram, who has been faithful in deed, "believed the Lord, and he counted it to him as righteousness." (Gen. 15:6) Because of Abram's distress and fear, God gives him a sign described in the rest of Genesis 15 as well as a dream foretelling the persecution of Abram's descendants in what would be the Hebrew enslavement in Egypt. God seals the deal when Abram wakes up by promising the land, naming the boundaries one by one, to Abram's offspring. The symbolic meaning of the ritual used in the dream is very clear: By God's initiative, not man's, God will keep His covenant. Famine, persecution, enslavement, and even disobedience will not interfere with His plan.

Let us take notice of three observations from Genesis 15:

- First, God makes it clear that most of his plan will not be fulfilled in Abram's lifetime. His plan has global proportions which will be acted on in His timing.

- Abram is told explicitly about an heir coming from his own body. He is promised offspring throughout these verses.

- There is no mention of Sarai.

What About Sarai?
In the midst of unanswered prayer, doubt, and longing; silence is maddening. We want answers and we want them fast. What is my place in God's plan? Specifically, what does he want me to do! Can

you imagine the turmoil Sarai must have endured during the ten years or so that elapsed between Genesis 15 and 16?

Let us journey back to the fateful night when Abram has the incredible encounter with God. The rescue of Lot and the aftermath was a time of anxiety for Abram and Sarai. Perhaps Abram has renewed hope and faith when he tells his wife of the subsequent vision he had from the Lord. Isn't it great for them to know that they are not abandoned! God has assured Abram that he will inherit the promised land of Canaan. He has also confirmed that Abram will have a son from his own loins. Oh, what wonderful news! Barrenness won't stop God. He has a plan. Everything will work out, in His own time of course!

So, as time goes on they both cling to the covenant revealed on that night. Abram is convinced that God has everything under control. But Sarai has her doubts off and on. Where is the promised child? Perhaps on occasion Sarai would ask her husband to recount his conversation with God.

Trying to conceal her desperation she might ask: "Are you sure he said there would be a child?"

"Yes," he assures her.

"From your own loins?" she asks.

"Certainly," he assures her.

"But Abram," she asks, "did God mention me?"

"Abram," she repeats, "did God say anything about me?" Abram's faltering answer would be, "No, Sarai." But don't read too much into that, he would try to reassure her, but what's the use. Sarai would have been seriously challenged to wait for God to provide a child!

The one thing Sarai is supposed to be able to do as a woman, she cannot seem to accomplish. No child, no promise fulfilled—no success. The one necessary and obvious thing to Sarai gets a blank response from God. Then Sarai begins to contrive a plan. It's not as if it isn't done by others. She knows a perfectly legitimate way to give Abram a child. And it would be a child that she could mother and he would have as an heir. That would solve everything. In fact, she rationalizes; this must have been God's intention all along!

So, here we have a woman who loves her husband, follows his leadership, trusts in God, but is obsessed with the one thing God has not yet made possible. Sound familiar? Do you and I do this on occasion? This could apply to any unanswered prayer or troubling circumstance out of our control. In their case, God has specified a plan and made it clear that he will fulfill the plan in his own time. All he asks is that they remain faithful. He asks the same of us. But of course, this isn't easy, because we are naturally prone to thinking that his plan must somehow revolve around our needs. Poor Sarai is not doing anything any of us can judge too harshly. She's just desperate. She uses this desperation to wear down her husband's resolve in Genesis 16.

We are told in verse 1 that Sarai had borne Abram no children. Meaning, things were not progressing as one might expect. The family of Abram is surely multiplying in other ways. They are probably prospering under Abraham's capable leadership. They are sojourning as commanded. But sadly, Sarai's identity and status is wrapped up in the one thing she cannot have or control! The plan she had probably been contriving for years revolved around her Egyptian servant Hagar. In 16:2, Sarai said to Abram, "'Behold now, the Lord has prevented me from bearing children. Go in to my servant; it may be that I shall obtain children by her.' And Abram listened to the voice of Sarai."

Like most women, Sarai was very perceptive. It was God indeed who had prevented her from bearing children. In womanlike fashion Sarai has been obsessing over the problem. Is this problem she perceives even a problem in the first place? No, not in the big picture, but she has lost all objectivity. She is perhaps frustrated, depressed, and feels cheated. In other words, she is focused on herself. She wants it resolved and I believe begins to wear down Abram's resolve to wait on God by pressuring him with her emotions. I say this because of two things: that's typical female behavior; and 16:2-3 says that "Abram listened to the voice of Sarai." Hebrew scholars say that this Hebrew word for voice is that same word for bleating sheep. This implies that Sarai wore Abram out with her constant emotional pleas. Therefore, "after Abram had lived ten years in the land of Canaan, Sarai, Abram's wife, took Hagar the Egyptian, her servant, and gave her to Abram her husband as a wife." Who is the initiator of this plan? Sarai. Who does Abram have to listen to for years pleading with him to follow her idea? Sarai. Who carries out the plan with what seems like a kind of formal custom? Sarai, with Abram's cooperation. Who should Abram have listened to instead? God, of course!

We women are often heard saying we just wish our husbands would listen to us. "If he would just listen to me. If only he could meet my needs or just take my advice." Okay, Sarai had that quality in her husband. He cherished her. And I think, in her self-focused crisis, she abused her husband's love. We women need to be careful of demanding and expecting unrealistic things from our men. The voice they must first listen to is the voice of God. That is hard to do when we become bleating sheep. If this could be true of Sarai, who demonstrates great strength and godliness at other times, it can be true of us all.

Like most women, Sarai was very perceptive in identifying the problems in her life. She was right in observing that God had prevented her from bearing children. In learning from Sarai's mistakes, we all would do well to make our theology bigger than our problems! Analyzing problems is not enough. Knowing he is sovereign is not enough. We must yield everyday to his wisdom and plan for our lives. We must daily obey His commands and wait on Him when there is no godly solution in the face of unanswered prayer. That is what faith is all about!

"As You Please"
I think Abram must have learned some severe lessons from the sin of not trusting God to give him a child thrzough his wife Sarai. Just read Genesis 16 in its brief entirety. Their household never completely recovers from the disaster! As pertains to Sarai, her brilliant plan did not turn out as she expected. As soon as Hagar

realized that this promotion to wife and mother would not truly enhance her status in the household, she became contemptuous towards Sarai. Perhaps she was hoping to replace Sarai completely. Even so, why should she be thrilled about being a surrogate mother!

In verse 5 Sarai says to her husband, "May the wrong done to me be on you! I gave my servant to your embrace, and when she saw that she had conceived, she looked on me with contempt. May the Lord judge between you and me!" But then Abram assures his wife, "'Behold, your servant is in your power; do to her as you please.' [Sarai still has authority from her husband to deal with the mess she created.] Then Sarai dealt harshly with her, and she fled from her."

A careful reading of this passage shows that things are happening on several levels. Sarai is mad that no one appreciates her personal sacrifice. Albeit, the sacrifice she begged to make! She didn't anticipate that this might lead to something else. I also speculate that Hagar's contempt of Sarai made Sarai suspect Abram's loyalty to her. A loyalty she put quite a strain on to say the least! Most importantly, Sarai is blaming her husband for following her advice! How female!! The moral of this story is: don't sin, even if it is culturally acceptable. Sin may look manageable at first, but it always takes you where you do not want to go! This blotch on Sarai and Abram's record took on a life of its own and was completely unnecessary.

After being assured by her husband that Hagar is still just a servant and placing the responsibility on her to make reparations, Sarai deals with her harshly. This may have meant that Hagar had to go back to doing light house work as Sarai's personal maid, or was informed of her inferior status to Sarai. A status or role affirmed later by God in Genesis 21:12. One thing stands out as obvious: Hagar and Sarai are enemies. While Sarai has the authority, Hagar has the child. Now the tables are turned by Abram's endorsement of Sarai's authority and Hagar flees from Sarai who once again has the upper hand.

Is this the same Sarah to whom Peter refers in 1 Peter 3? Is this the way a holy woman behaves? Let's just say Abraham and his wife make big mistakes here and live to pay the price. Some would say Sarai seems vengeful, some might say protective of her marriage. She thought she was doing something good in using Hagar as a surrogate mother. Hagar tried to turn the tables against her. There is no getting away from the sinfulness of this domestic arrangement. Remember, sin has a way of taking you where you don't want to go!

In Galatians 4:23 we are told that the son born of a slave woman (Hagar) was born according to the flesh, while the son of the free woman (Sarah) was born through promise. God protects Sarai and affirms her role as Abraham's wife and the mother of his true heir. She is called holy in 1 Peter 3. She is Abram's cherished princess. Abraham is not told by God that his child will come specifically through Sarah until later in Genesis 17:19 and 18:10. Nor is there any record of God speaking directly to her as He does with Abraham. Interestingly enough, God does descend to the lowly servant Hagar.

God Loves Sarai's Enemy
In Genesis 16:7 "the angel of the Lord" (theologians believe this phrase to be a reference to the second person of the trinity, Jesus, making a preincarnate, earthly appearance) finds Hagar at a spring of water in the wilderness. He addresses her as "Hagar, servant of Sarai." There are two main points to derive from this encounter between God and Hagar. First, God loves our enemies while still loving us! There are hints throughout that God sympathizes with Sarai because she is Abram's true wife. But he still cares for Hagar and finds her in the wilderness after she has run away. He comforts her with the promise that she too will produce many offspring as a result of her son Ishmael. She is told by God to call her son Ishmael because it means "God hears"! He hears Hagar in her distress and speaks to her directly. Not a privilege afforded to many. He also gives her a vision of who her son will be and what

he will be like. He comforts in a practical way.

Secondly, God doesn't let people off the hook just because He shows them grace! God is honest with Hagar about her son. He tells her that he will be an outcast. He also gives her a simple command at the very beginning: "return to your mistress and submit to her" (v. 9). She must go back and face the mess she left behind. She played a willing role and now must endure the chaos she's helped to make. In so doing she will be providing her son with a father. Does Hagar resent God's frank prophecy or harsh command? Is she like contemporary women who think they are being mistreated when given the unvarnished truth? No! Genesis 16:13 tells us how grateful Hagar is for God's tough compassion: "You are a God of seeing; truly I have seen Him who looks after me." Now she knows that Yaweh is her friend too.

The Vision Reborn
Abram was eighty six when Hagar bore Ishmael to him. For thirteen years Abram fathers his son and teaches him. For thirteen years Sarai has to live with not only her barrenness, but Hagar's fulfillment in motherhood. Maybe during this time Sarai was depressed while Hagar gloated a bit. Likely, Abram was a loving father. The couple may have had strained relations. Could this have been a spiritually dry season as well? We can only imagine the injured family dynamics for all the parties. We only know from Scripture that thirteen years elapsed.

Then once again, at over ninety nine years of age, Abram hears from God in Genesis 17:1-6 "'I am God Almighty; walk before me, and be blameless, that I may make my covenant between me and you, and may multiply you greatly.' Then Abram fell on his face and God said to him, 'Behold, my covenant is with you and you shall be the father of a multitude of nations. No longer shall your name be called Abram, but your name shall be Abraham, for I have made you the father of a multitude of nations.'"

God proceeds to reaffirm what Abraham already knows from past encounters with God. He will be blessed, defended, and fruitful in this God-initiated covenant. He then carefully lays out for Abraham a procedure called circumcision which he commands him to carry out on every living male in his household.

Resolve to Obey
In Genesis 17:14 God changes Abram's name to Abraham and steps up the level of commitment for Abraham by requiring not only faithfulness but obedience to a very specific command to circumcise every living male in his household. This is followed by some very serious stuff in 17:15-16, "And God said to Abraham, 'As for Sarai your wife, you shall not call her name Sarai, but Sarah shall be her name. I will bless her, and moreover, I will give you a son by her, and she shall become nations; kings of peoples shall come from her.'" Abraham's response is to fall on his face, laugh, and say to himself, "Shall a child be born to a man who is a hundred years old? Shall Sarah, who is ninety years old, bear a child?" He also expresses a wish for Ishmael to be included in the plan—an idea that God immediately rejects. Rather, his wife Sarah will bear him a son named Isaac. In this whimsical and tender exchange Abraham is assured that all he has been waiting for is soon to be delivered.

The faithful and forgiven Abraham immediately carries out God's command to circumcise. No doubt circumcising hundreds of men was a bloody and unpleasant business. In light of the promises just made by God to Abraham, is it too much to imagine that Abraham felt energized and renewed even as he carried out this vast undertaking?

God has rewarded Abraham and Sarah with new names to symbolize his affirmation. He has validated Sarah as the future mother of Isaac, which Abraham and Sarah might not have been certain of until now. They might have thought they had been disqualified because of their failure with Hagar. God has reminded Abraham that he has more to do for him and that the covenant not only still stands, but is moving forward. He assures Abraham that Ishmael is not a mistake, but also part of his sovereign plan.

And to top it all off God publishes the birth announcement of Isaac one year before birth. Even before conception!

A Divine Visit

All of this leads up to another even more amazing encounter between Abraham and God. We are told in verse 1 that "the Lord appeared to him by the Oaks of Mamre, as he sat at the door of his tent in the heat of the day." In a place from which the patriarch could keep watch over his family, Abraham has a sort of siesta, perhaps recovering from the ordeal of circumcision. Moses tells the reader very clearly that Abraham's encounter is with God. Verses 2 through 21 would be very puzzling were it not for the clarity of verse 22 and 19:1. Evidently, God, in some bodily form is accompanied by two angels who are also in the likeness of men.

Notice Abraham's eager reverence toward the three men he sees in verse 2. He runs to meet them and bows. They have come to him, yet he bows to them! He seems to recognize the importance of his visitors. He implores them to stay and immediately enlists Sarah's help to bake three cakes. While eating her cakes, they ask about Sarah. Why do they ask about her? Think about all the excitement from Abraham and his elaborate welcome. Isn't it strange that Sarah would prepare the cakes and do her part without coming out to personally greet the guests? Even if she didn't perceive that she was entertaining God and two angels, wouldn't it be fitting for Abraham's princess to be a little friendlier?

When Abraham tells them that she is in the tent, the Lord says in verse 10: "I will surely return to you about this time next year, and Sarah your wife shall have a son." Then verse 11 explains the background as if this has to do with Sarah's reasoning (because obviously the reader knows their background!). Abraham is old, she is old. She has long quit trying to have children. And perhaps Abraham was too busy circumcising, or too afraid to tell his wife about that last talk with God. If a woman has totally given up on her dreams and believes she has been forsaken, how available would she be for her husband? Some of this is speculative, but how else do we explain the need for God Himself to tell Sarah that she will bear Abraham's son, that she is not forsaken?

Is Anything Too Hard For The Lord?
I think Sarah was afraid to face God. Either she didn't think she deserved to see him or she was afraid to be disappointed again. When Sarah heard the Lord's words she reacted much the same way as her husband did earlier. In verse 1 Sarah laughs to herself, saying, "After I am worn out, and my lord is old, shall I have pleasure?" The Lord said to Abraham, "Why did Sarah laugh and say, 'Shall I indeed bear a child, now that I am old?' Is anything too hard for the Lord? At the appointed time I will return to you about this time next year, and Sarah shall have a son." But Sarah did not want to disappoint God. She denies her own laughter and God corrects her.

Much has been made of Sarah's laughter. That she has such a great sense of irony makes her interesting. Is Sarah bitter or without faith as some might assume? I think she is just tired of hoping and waiting. She is weary of being a barren disappointment for all her famed beauty. Sarah may not have lost faith in God, only in what he can do with her. Do you feel like Sarah? Have you failed God and felt discarded? Do you know what it's like to stop hoping for the answered prayer? Are you certain you are not worthy of God's promises? Well guess what Sarah? It is not about your success or worthiness anyway! The whole time it has been about God and His power. What a relief for Sarah if this led to renewal in her marriage.

God's Steadfast Justice
God has blessed Sarai/Sarah with exceptional beauty and youthfulness. He has used her appearance to bring glory to Himself. He has blessed Abraham with a woman who entrances kings. Sarah has what on the surface appears to be an excess of vitality and good looks considering her barrenness. Now she has been assured of God's purposes in all this. All of the blessings and

waiting for answered prayer are leading up to a preordained time.

In the following verses God actually confides in Abraham his plans to destroy Sodom. He is interested in Abraham's input and in demonstrating to him his righteousness and justice. It is as if Abraham's role to "command his children and his household to keep the way of the Lord by doing righteousness and justice" is a reason for God to set a very real example of that very thing in Sodom and Gomorrah. Abraham has a good sense of God's power. He is fearful for his family in Sodom and is humbly motivated by compassion. So God encourages and allows Abraham to question and challenge his plans. God's plans hold up to Abraham's scrutiny. Even more amazingly, God entertains Abraham's negotiations to spare as many righteous as possible. From this account we learn about the compassion of Abraham and God. We learn that God's justice is tempered with love.

Genesis 18 recounts Abraham and Sarah's personal, revelatory, and intimate visit with God himself. If there was any doubt on Sarah's part about finally bearing a child, this was the time to resolve it. If Abraham is concerned about his nephew Lot's fate, this was the time to speak up. God came to them on their turf, in His time.

It seems that the two men who accompanied the Lord to visit with Abraham are the angels who went into Sodom in 19:1.

A Fatal Visit
Lot is visited by angels who are on a rescue mission. There are some interesting comparisons between Lot's visit and Abraham's. It is clear that Lot recognizes that his two visitors are deserving of respect. He offers hospitality. He prepares a feast, but there is no mention of his wife yet. It is also obvious that his hospitality is laced with fear. He has a sense that his guests must be protected. He knows that his town is not safe. He values the stunning angel's safety even more than his own daughters whom he would rather have raped than the angels. Please note in 19:6-7 that Lot made this offer of his daughters to the men of his city with the door

closed behind him. Was he trying to hide the decadence of his environs from the angels? Was he afraid of his wife and daughters hearing his disgusting cowardice?

We can learn a lot about the progression of sin's hold on our lives by watching Lot. Was this Lot a different man from the one who entered the scene after choosing such prime real estate? Here he is now, living in the heart of the city, hanging out at the town gate, and offering his own daughters to a mob of perverts. Their reply to his proposition: "Stand back! This fellow came to sojourn, and he has become the judge! Now we will deal worse with you than with them." So the all the men of his town proceeded to crush Lot and break his door down. It must have been a very strong door! If it weren't for the angels reaching out to grab him, slamming shut the door, and rendering the mob blind, Lot and his family would have been destroyed. This is a prime example of sin taking you where you don't want to go!

The Outcry
The theme of God's love tempered justice is never more apparent than in 18:20 when the Lord refers to the outcry against the cities which he will verify and 19:13 in which the angels do verify the need for destruction. God makes clear to Abraham that He is responding to an outcry against Sodom and Gomorrah. Their sin is not just a matter of breaking God's laws. The sin of this community is a matter of grief and suffering to their fellow man. The outcry of anguish from victims motivates God. Sodom's destruction actually begins with its own sinful behavior. God will destroy the cities only after He has demonstrated his own faithfulness to Abraham and willingness to be compassionate. The deal between God and Abraham to rescue the righteous is a mark of God's compassion.

The Rescue of the Reluctant
In Genesis 19:17 the angels seize Lot and his family and tells them to escape to the mountains. Because of fear, Lot first refuses

to make the journey. He bargains for an easier escape route to a nearby small town. In verse 21, one of the men, or angels, responds to Lots' plea with a promise that he will not overthrow the town of Zoar. He promises not to begin the destruction of Sodom and Gomorrah until Lot arrives there. In verse 3 we see that Lot comes to Zoar, and then the Lord rains fire and brimstone on Sodom and Gomorrah; the valley and all the inhabitants of the cities, and the vegetation. But Lot's wife "looks back" in verse 6 and is destroyed as well. Was she turned into a pillar of salt because she struggled behind in disobedience, reluctant to leave her comfortable home? Was she in denial of the severity of their situation? Unable to move forward with her family, Lot's wife became baggage. The compromise of Lot in moving to a godless location was devastating for his family. Since the only reference to Lot's wife is rather negative, it seems she left her heart behind in sinful Sodom.

In verse 27 I am struck by the image of Abraham overlooking all of the smoke and desolation of the cities in which Lot had lived. In this very place God spoke to him and revealed his plans for annihilation. From that very place he sees the awesome destructive force of God. Yet, God has spared Abraham's family, including Lot. "God remembered Abraham and sent him out of the midst of the overflow." An act of compassion coupled with brimstone and fire; a powerful combination from Almighty God.

Lot and His Daughters
In verse 27 we see that Lot is not so enthralled with God's power and compassion. Instead he is acting out of fear. He is a dispossessed city dweller who needs a place to hide and lick his wounds. The small town he persuaded God not to destroy does not feel safe enough to him. So he flees to the mountains with his daughters. They trade the safe haven God provided for a cave. Like many of us, when crisis strikes, instead of praising God for sparing our lives and trusting him for the future, we flee to our own spiritual cave. This isolation may be the thing that led

to the desperation of Lot's daughters. They each sinned against their father by getting him drunk and having sex with him. Their behavior was out of the fear that came from seeing their father hide in a cave instead of being a spiritual leader. Their mother certainly didn't set an example of faithfulness to God. They follow suit with desperate scheming.

On their journey they would have seen total destruction everywhere. Isolated in a cave they don't know if there are any survivors apart from those few in Zoar. Their father is fearful and unstable. I would speculate that in the mind of the older sister a father's help would be necessary to venture out. The thought of surviving this far only to die as old women in a cave would be gut wrenching. Father is becoming more physically and mentally unstable everyday. Then a plan begins to take form. The elder tells the younger sister about it and she agrees. There is no need to let the family just die off. They agree to take turns getting their father drunk (wine being one provision he made sure of) and sleeping with him. The resulting pregnancies will ensure that their lives still have hope and purpose. So, they carry out the plan, believing this is the only solution, and eventually leave the caves with sons who start new civilizations—Moab and Ben-Ammi.

Nothing excuses the sin of Lot's daughters. Evil has a way of convincing us of its necessity. They were weakened by their father's frailty. Lot's daughters did not have a strong and godly leader as Sarah did. Perhaps their sin was also prompted by bitterness towards a father who was earlier willing to sacrifice them to the sadistic perverts on the eve of Sodom's destruction. I doubt if this escaped their memory.

In Genesis 20 Abraham journeys again to a new territory. There is no further mention of Lot. Lot will always be remembered as the man who chose to put his family in jeopardy and was tricked into impregnating his daughters. Yet God saved him. God was faithful to a man who had compromised his witness for the sake of Abraham. He was faithful to Abraham who had pleaded for Lot. Even in the face of man's failures, God's will is still sovereign.

Abraham and Abimelech

It will be necessary to carefully read Genesis 20 before continuing. Again we see Abraham faced with the predicament of a beautiful wife while sojourning in Gerar. When presumably searched and questioned, Abraham said of his wife, "She is my sister." Once again Sarah and Abraham are unified in their trust in God. Sarah follows her husband's leadership by saying she is his sister as indicated in verse 5. Abimelech, the king of Gerar, sends for and takes Sarah into his home. God comes to Abimelech in a dream and says, "Behold, you are a dead man because of the woman whom you have taken, for she is a man's wife" (v. 3). In summary, Abimelech pleads to God for mercy on the grounds that his deed was not intentional; God lets him know the way out: give back the woman he unknowingly stole from Abraham or else face death. In fact what God specifically says to the king in verse 7 is incredible: "Now then, return the man's wife, for he is a prophet, so that he will pray for you, and you shall live. But if you do not return her, know that you shall surely die, you, and all who are yours."

God informs Abimelech that everything is under His control. He knows that Abimelech was ignorant of Sarah being Abraham's wife. God knows that Abimelech has not touched her yet because God was the one who prevented him from committing this sin! God actually expects Abimelech to return Sarah to her husband and wait for prayer and healing in return from the husband! As in Genesis 12 there is nothing said by God or the text to indicate God's displeasure with his prophet. In fact, God validates Abraham to Abimelech.

One of the most puzzling observations to be made about this chapter is the comment from Abraham to Abimelech in verse 12: "She is indeed my sister, the daughter of my father though not the daughter of my mother, and she became my wife." My question is: Why does the text now indicate that Abraham and Sarah have not really been lying all along—that she is both his sister and his wife? Why now? Stay with me on this for what I believe to be the answer.

First, let's eliminate possible wrong answers. One might be tempted to see Abraham's comment as a lie. This is implausible since there is nothing within the text to correct Abraham or inform the reader that this is not a true statement of his relationship with Sarah. Furthermore, precedent for some incest within Abraham's family is set in Genesis 11:29. A second possible interpretation I have heard is that perhaps Abraham is telling the truth, but for the purpose of rationalizing some sin on his part. My answer to this is simple: There are no textual indicators in Genesis 12 or here in Genesis 20 to indicate any displeasure on God's part with Abraham. Apart from pop-Christian interpretations, there is nothing here for Abraham to rationalize.

Though many modern day speakers and authors would say the opposite, I see Abraham's actions as part of a plan to preserve his family for the purpose of staying true to his call from God. I see Sarah's obedience, not as something for which God will have to excuse or punish, but rather as the very thing Peter commends as submitting to her husband and not fearing the frightening thing (1 Peter 3:1-6). How could Sarah be commended for going along with Abraham on this if his actions were wrong? I can't find any scriptural precedent for such thinking.

I think a clue to the bottom line here is found in Abraham's remarks to Abimelech concerning the true nature of his relationship with Sarah. Look at verse 10 when Abimelech asks Abraham why he has brought about the conflict. "What did you see, that you did this thing?" In other words, "What is your reasoning for allowing me to take your beloved and beautiful wife?" Or, the underlying question: "Why are you so different from all other men?" Abraham refers to God in the next three verses twice. He tells the king about leaving his father's home and attributes it to God. When he admits to his fear about entering Gerar, it is attributed to the lack of fear of God in that land. Additionally, he points out his wife's spirit of submission by referring to her willingness to say she is his sister. She apparently did this as a "kindness" to her husband. As far as Abraham seems to be concerned, this whole thing is about something bigger than his marriage. Their withholding of their marriage relationship is not the point in all this. That's why it doesn't come out until now when Abimelech is inquiring. Abraham's strategy is about God. The One True God who is not known to the culture around Abraham. The bottom line is about Abraham trusting God to bring him and Sarah through as examples of His power.

As an act of restitution, Abimelech gives to Abraham sheep, oxen, male and female servants. He returns Sarah to Abraham and gives them permission to live wherever they please in his country. He then gives an interesting sort of apology to Sarah. He tells her that a gift of a thousand pieces of silver to Abraham is a sign of her innocence before all. He respects them. He fears Abraham's God. Then, in verse 17, Abraham prays for Abimelech and heals his family so that they will bear children. "For the Lord had closed all the wombs of the house of Abimelech because of Sarah, Abraham's wife." So now, in Gerar, there is at least one household that does fear God. It is the household of the king. This king and those around him will know of Abraham and his God. They will remember the power of God through Abraham and his beautifully submissive wife. They may not understand or believe or obey Abraham's God. But they know not to mess with Him. This has been the consistent bottom line throughout Abraham's life.

In Genesis 1 the Lord visits Sarah as promised and she conceives and bears a son to Abraham in his old age. Not only will Abraham believe Isaac is his child, but everyone in their region will have heard about the episode with Abimelech and know of Sarah's vindication. Her devotion and faithfulness to her husband will be unquestioned! God's fulfillment of the promise of a son to this woman past childbearing years will be known!

Laughter: Good and Bad
God had previously named their child Isaac (meaning "he laughs") in 18:17-19. As commanded, Abraham circumcised his son when

he was eight days old. It is lovely to read Sarah's praise remarks in 21:6-7: "God has made laughter for me; everyone who hears will laugh over me. Who would have said to Abraham that Sarah would nurse children? Yet I have born him a son in his old age." Sarah is delighted. Her happiness would never have been so great if the child had not been a miracle. When God gives Isaac to Sarah and Abraham he gives them back their laughter. Not just the chuckle of derision, but a clear and free expression of joy.

Another type of laughter was soon to be heard in their household. On the day that Isaac was weaned (around three years old) his dad throws him a big party. According to 21:9, "Sarah saw the son of Hagar the Egyptian, whom she had borne to Abraham, laughing. So she said to Abraham, 'Cast out this slave woman with her son, for the son of this slave woman shall not be heir with my son Isaac.'"

Ishmael would be fourteen at this point. The "laughter" referred to in verse 9 probably means laughing in mockery. Ishmael's mockery of Isaac, who is a toddler, possibly stems from his mother's attitude. Was she fueling the hope in Ishmael that his father would choose him to be the heir? If so, this would be in horrible contempt for all that Abraham has endured. The report of this mockery at a feast in honor of the one being mocked is probably reflective of Hagar and Ishmael's over all attitudes. I don't believe Sarah is just outraged about one incident, but about the contempt for Isaac that is breeding inside of Ishmael and his mother.

Sarah's Demand
Sarah takes the problem straight to Abraham. She is not meek or sweet or even subtle. She is a submissive woman who has earned the right to make an occasional demand. If we post modern women were to adorn ourselves with the gentle and quiet spirit towards our husbands on a daily basis like Sarah, then we might also amass a power in crisis similar to hers when she makes a rare demand. Sarah's words, "Cast out this slave woman with

her son, for the son of this slave woman shall not be heir with my son Isaac," was a call to action for Abraham. Perhaps he had been denying to himself that there was a problem. No doubt he loved Ishmael and felt guilty that he couldn't be the heir. In fact, his keeping Ishmael with him might have been enough to delude Hagar into false hopes.

In verses 11 and 12 Abraham takes this matter to God. He does what every godly woman should want from her husband. He listens to God first. Previously, in 16:b Abraham listened to Sarah and it got them all in this mess. This time he listens to God and gets verification first. God tells Abraham, "whatever Sarah says to you, do as she tells you, for through Isaac shall your offspring be named." God only refers to Hagar as the slave woman. In God's eyes only Sarah is validated as the wife.

It is sad to read in 21:14-21 the suffering endured by Hagar and her son. She was not innocent or a total victim. Rather, she played a willing part in trying to take advantage of her mistress's barrenness and usurp her. Her lot of remaining a servant whose son would not be the heir (though he was raised by his father) was not accepted gracefully. I think Hagar is not painted in the most positive light by Scripture, though she is not by any means the only one to blame.

Based on all God has thus far told Abraham about his family and who would be and bear his heir, I believe that Hagar and Ishmael are leaving in God's timing. The incident at the feast in Genesis 1 is just the impetus God used to bring it about. It had already been ordained by God that Ishmael would be the founder of another nation. It is sad that there had to be such bitterness, but the dispute over his mockery of Isaac was not ultimately the cause of their exile. It was simply part of God's sovereign plan. As harsh as it seems to see the mother and son sent off into the wilderness (which was at God's command, not just Sarah's), the two are once again met by God. God led them to water, and was with Ishmael as he grew up. His compassion is always around the corner, but his will is never thwarted!

Gracious In His Dealings

Now, let's take a look at an interesting encounter between Abraham and his former rival, Abimelech in Genesis 21:22-34. As you recall in chapter 20, the previous meeting between Abraham and Abimelech was humbling for Abimelech and victorious for Abraham. From the moment the drama began between the two, the one with position and authority held very little real power, while the obscure nomad held all the cards. Abraham's power was in his mighty God. Abimelech seems not to have forgotten the great advantages of Abraham and demonstrates respect, even fear, during this confrontation.

It seems that Abraham refused to back down and complains to Abimelech when some of his servants seize a well and prevent him from using it. Abimelech claims ignorance when informed that he has offended Abraham. He remembers what happened last time. Abraham promises (vvs. 23-24) not to deal too harshly with Abimelech. Abraham initiates a covenant with Abimelech by graciously making a gift of sheep and goats to him. The gift of seven ewes is an indication on Abraham's part that he dug the well. Remember, Abimelech had previously promised Abraham that he would be allowed to sojourn freely in Gerar. It is likely that the king brought his commander along because he feared a war with Abraham. Or perhaps the commander was warned by Abraham during the seizing of the well to go fetch the king!

So what has been accomplished here? Abraham and his large family will be respected and unharrassed. The name of God will continue to grow in fame. People like Abimelech and other rulers will have this message reinforced: Don't mess with Abraham because he worships a Great God—One who is both mighty in power and gracious in his dealings with men.

The Sacrifice

Sarah is truly blessed with a godly husband. He listens to God first. When God calls Abraham by name in Gen. he answers with the now famed words, "Here am I". The task at hand that day was not any easier than the others, in fact harder. A task Sarah may not have been told about. God said, "Take your son, your only son Isaac, whom you love, and go to the land of Moriah, and offer him there as a burnt offering on one of the mountains of which I shall tell you." Every indication is that Abraham obeyed God without hesitation. He was prepared to carry out this command. We are not told how he felt. Of course he wouldn't have been pleased. But he might have known God had something great in store for them. The journey to Mount Moriah would have taken about three days. Perhaps Abraham explained to Isaac the purpose of the journey. Perhaps his relationship with Isaac was so strong and grounded in trust that the boy was willing in his part. But I'm sure he trusted his father's love and submitted. That's what he'd seen his mother model all of his life. So Abraham carried out orders certain that "the Lord will provide". And He did! Abraham's obedience was greatly blessed by God.

The New Testament commentary on Abraham in Hebrews 11:17-19 tells us that this command to sacrifice Isaac was a test. Abraham was so trusting and certain of the power of God that he "considered that God was able even to raise him from the dead...." I believe on the way to Mount Moriah Abraham was saying goodbye to his son. He was giving up to God the person and idea he loved the most. His identity would not be wrapped up in God's blessings and promises. His identity would be found in God himself. Abraham was recognizing the right of Yaweh to give and take. And if God demands even the very promise and blessing He's bestowed upon his servant, it will be given him gladly. Figuratively speaking Abraham did receive Isaac back from the dead.

After all that Abraham has been through, after all the faith and obedience he has demonstrated, God wants to lead him to the next level! Notice that this test from God is something that Abraham must face alone. Only after obeying God and following all necessary preparation for the sacrifice (Gen. 22:9-14) the angel of the Lord stopped Abraham from carrying out the sacrifice. The

Lord provided Abraham with a substitute sacrifice; a ram, to offer in place of Isaac.

Sarah's part in this is unknown to us. I can't imagine that Abraham would have thought it prudent to tell her! I see Abraham as a man who is capable of walking this road alone with God. Sarah was married to a man who could communicate intimately with God and be trusted to obey his most challenging call yet. Because of her loyalty to and trust of Abraham, Sarah could stay in bed and sleep away the morning without a worry. Her husband may have returned with a victorious account of God's sovereign grace. Wives like Sarah have the luxury of husbands like Abraham who take care of business.

Faith in the Future

Genesis 23:1 tells us that Sarah lived one hundred and twenty seven years. After her death Abraham took another wife, Keturah, and had several concubines. Though there are differing views on this perplexing aspect of Abraham's life; I have a two-part explanation. First, Abraham has been told by God that he will be the father of a great nation and have many children. He knows that Isaac is the blessed inheritor of that covenant. Certainly, one husband, one wife is meant as God's ideal. But Abraham is also to produce many heirs for future dominance of the land. The difficulty lies in providing spouses for his children. It would be unthinkable for them to marry the Canaanites who inhabit the land. So, the second part of this is that Abraham solves the problem the way his father Terah solved it: by providing children from different mothers from which his sons can marry. Those sons will not be available for Isaac yet, hence the mission of Eliezer in Genesis 24:3-4 to find a wife (cousin) from among Abraham's people back in Mesopotamia (Remember that Sarah is Abraham's half-sister!).

This chapter details Abraham's negotiations to purchase for the full price a burial site for Sarah and the rest of his family. The Hittites who owned the land in this part of Canaan wanted to give the land to Abraham. A sojourner like Abraham could not easily purchase land in ancient Canaan. Any transactions he might possibly negotiate would not be legal without the consent of the "sons of Het." Abraham will not settle for a temporary burial site. He persists in his offer until it is accepted by all. His offer is probably ten times its value, but worth it to him because it gives him absolute title to his wife's resting place. It was more than just a grave to Abraham. This tells us that Abraham was willing to pay a huge price to honor Sarah. He knew his people would some day take possession and inhabit the land for good. I believe Abraham was honoring God and his progenitors with this extraordinary commitment to buy the field with the cave and the trees of the land in the presence of the Hittites.

Imperishable Beauty
What was the result of Sarah's submission? Was she weak or downtrodden as the feminists say? Was she a mere pawn in the hands of her husband? Or is there more to her submissive spirit than meets the eye? She did not really fit the conventional mold of being easily led. In fact, Sarah is far from simple; she is far more complicated than her role suggests.

Sarah trusted her husband's leadership in times of peril. When she could have panicked or argued she instead submitted to her husband. When she committed sin and led her husband astray, she kept the faith and endured anyway. When away from her husband and in the home of a pagan suitor, she trusted in God. We also know Sarah was a lioness about her son's welfare. She wasn't polarized by self doubt when her son needed defending. She knew how to state her case boldly and clearly and yet she is described by Peter as the model of a gentle and quiet spirit. The result of Sarah's submission was a life of faith, perseverance, and inspiration.

I'm sure her physical beauty was nice for Abraham, but it is not what kept him going. She was made beautiful to him by her submissive spirit: a spirit that said, "Okay, honey. Let's leave all we know to answer God's call." Sarah inspired her husband to be her "lord" by thinking of him as such (cf. 1 Peter 3:6), even when he wasn't perfect. Sarah sacrificed much for her husband yet never lost faith. At times there was an edge to Sarah that is often glossed over by those who oversimplify her. Sarah's pleasing appearance; submission to her husband; love and trust for her husband; protectiveness of her son; faith in God's power; sense of irony; and delight in God's faithfulness were God's ingredients for a holy woman. Not a perfect woman or simplistic woman, but a holy woman who serves as an example to all women.

Peter tells us that if we do well and do not fear anything that is frightening, we are Sarah's children. For today's woman, submission itself is the frightening thing. To be supportive and loving when we have been coached all our lives to compete with and demand from men, is not the cultural norm. Tending to a husband's needs when one doesn't feel like it is not exactly featured in women's magazines. To surrender one's need to take charge and fix everything won't come easily to those of us who have always believed in self reliance. Letting a husband take the reigns and make ourselves vulnerable can be daunting. But it does have its rewards.

Women like Sarah often have strong men who love them fiercely. They have men who fork over big bucks and make sacrifices to cherish them. Submissive women like Sarah can trust in God to work on their men. Wives with a gentle and quiet spirit know the secrets to getting their husband's attention. The list is endless.

Here are the secrets that holy women have used to inspire men to be happy leaders in the home physically, verbally, and spiritually.

Physical

- Serving your husband's needs when he comes home from work is a way of giving life. A snack, a cold beverage, his favorite dinner and some quiet time will make him feel like an honored guest and look forward to coming home. Save complaints, advice, and nagging for later. Much later.

- Look your best for him on a consistent basis. Whatever you usually look like is the picture he will have in his mind.

- Back rubs and foot rubs. If you must talk to him about something important he will be a captive audience!

- Never withhold intimacy to punish your husband for being "insensitive." Be available and loving even when you are tired and not in the mood. Marital intimacy is not always romantic, it is just good therapy!

- Realize that marital intimacy is the primary way women can give of themselves to their husbands. It is selfish not to extend yourself, just as it is also depriving yourself!

Verbal

- Welcome your husband home without immediately treating his arrival as your childcare reinforcement.

- Treat your husband like a man, not like a child. Don't talk to him the way women in commercials or sitcoms talk to or about their husbands. Be sweet and respectful.

- If your husband toils daily at a stressful job or even hates his job, cut him some slack when he comes home. He is showing you he loves you by the very fact that he goes to that job everyday! Don't expect the man you married to talk to you or listen to you in the same way a girl friend would. You married a man not another woman!

- If your husband needs encouragement, don't waste much time on words. Put the kids to bed and show him that you think he is wonderful. Sexual intimacy is the number one way to let your man know that you love him. It will inspire him to succeed. Intimacy will help make him forget a bad day at work. It will cause him to appreciate you.

- Compliment all the little things your husband does. "Thanks so much for changing the light bulb!" "Honey, thanks so much for leading our family in grace at meals." "I just love to see you playing with the kids." "Thanks for this wonderful necklace!" Even if you don't like it, encourage his gesture. You want to encourage those efforts, knowing that they will improve over time if he gets positive results!

- Don't react to problems with emotional outbursts or accusatory language. Talk calmly and address problems with a tone of respect and dignity. Wait for a neutral time when possible.

- Be funny and playful whenever possible! Laugh at his jokes!

Spiritual

- Pray for God's will in your husband's life. Let him know that you care most about him pleasing God, not you!

- Every time you feel tempted to indulge in sinful fantasies pray for your husband.

- Ask him to hold you accountable for something you need to improve in your character or lifestyle. (Even ask him what he thinks needs improving!)

- Behave in a way that suggests to your man that you love and want his leadership.

- Give your husband to God. Trust God to lead your husband. Avoid giving your husband unsolicited advice.

- Don't encroach upon his God-given role as provider and father of the family, even if he is a reluctant leader.

Unless a man is an absolute jerk, he will be inspired by a daughter of Sarah. He will be affected by his wife's attitude to live up to his calling as leader. In the absence of nagging and hostility he will be free to hear God calling his name. Even if you have to wait forty years for big results, you will know that you have glorified God and been an example to your children!

Sarah's Silhouette
Earlier I posed the question, "What does it look like to be a holy woman?" The profile of a holy woman has always been varied and unique to her personality and family. She makes herself beautiful by loving and inspiring the leadership of her husband. The holy woman is more concerned about the hidden person of the heart than the image seen by the world. She is less and less charmed by frivolous romance, and more and more desirous of spiritual depth. She has calm in her soul that generates confidence. She radiates back to her family the joy of the Lord. This is what makes her appealing to her husband.

Sarah's message to wives is simple, but not easy. There are frightening things ahead for all women, but the daughters of Sarah won't succumb to fear. Like Sarah, she fears nothing as much as disappointing God. With such clarity, all other priorities fall into place. As we teach each other, pray together, and trust in God, we can live according to His grace and not fear!

Questions for Study and Discussion:

1. Would following a call from God be easier for you to obey if you personally received it or if it came through your husband? (If you are not married, then think of this hypothetically)

2. Abraham was a great visionary leader. What might be the challenges and blessings of his gifts for his wife?

3. What do you think of the author's comment that "women flourish under the love and affirmation of a strong leader"?

4. Based on 1 Peter 2:12, how does God's desire to bring fame to His name still perpetuate to this day? How does our submission to this bring Him glory?

5. What are some lessons to be learned from Sarai's "solution" to the problem of barrenness? Even though the cultural specifics are hard to relate to, are there things about Sarai's situation that make her obsession understandable. How do you relate to Sarai?

6. Do you agree with the author that we women tend to blame others (in particular, our husbands) for our mistakes? Please explain, especially in light of our modern culture of feminism.

7. Turn to Gen. 16:7-16 to read the account of God speaking to Hagar. List specific ways God encouraged Hagar. Then list her responses.

8. Turn to 1 Peter and answer the following:

   In 2:21-25 we have a description of Jesus' willing sacrifice. I Peter 3 tells wives to have the same spirit of submission toward their husbands. Read through 1Peter 3:7.

   When Jesus was undergoing trial and crucifixion, to whom was he submitting? Explain.

In the case of a Christian wife, to whom is she submitting?

In I Peter 3:1-7 what are the benefits for a woman who submits? What might the benefits be for her husband?

Based on the context of this passage in I Peter, what is the basis for godly submission in marriage?

In these verses Peter talks about external adornments as opposed to the adorning of the hidden person of the heart. How might the two sometimes compliment or at other times interfere with each other?

Do these verses mean to ban the use of beauty products or accessories? What is Peter's emphasis?

Notice that Peter's instructions are to wives first, then to husbands. Any theories on why that is? Does this imply that there is something men need from their wives before they can really do verse 7 well?

9. Please turn to Romans 4:1-3. Abraham believed God. That belief counted for a lot to God! Now turn to John 3:16-21. Make a list of the key things this passage tells us to believe.

10. In Genesis 15 we are told that Abraham believed God for something very specific. It was important enough for God to count it to him as righteousness. Can you name the specific thing God wanted Abraham to believe? You'll need to read at least 15:1-6

God wanted Abraham to totally trust that He would fulfill his promise for a son. He didn't want Abraham to live according to what he could see now, but according to God's unseen promise. Doesn't he ask the same of us? God rewarded Abraham for his faith by giving him further revelation concerning his offspring. Abraham would know that God's plan was global and independent of human involvement.

NAOMI AND RUTH: AN OASIS OF FAITHFULNESS

Scripture References:
Ruth ◆ Matthew 1:5

In the historically turbulent days when the judges ruled the land of Israel, there was famine. The famine which Naomi and her husband Elimelech fled was one of pestilence and starvation. Yet another famine was sweeping through the land of Israel at that time: one of unfaithfulness to the God of Israel. In the book of Ruth we have the refreshing story of two women who are devoted to each other and God in a way that is beyond what anyone in their ancient culture—or ours—would expect. Despite calamity after calamity, Naomi trusts in God and yearns to get back to Bethlehem. Her faith inspires Ruth whose own faith and loyalty in turn make an indelible impression on all of Bethlehem.

Our story begins with a man of Bethlehem in Judah who takes his family from the famine in Bethlehem to sojourn in the country of Moab. Elimelech, his wife Naomi and their two sons Mahlon ("puny") and Chilion ("pining") become temporary residents, leaving the culture they know and the property they own to eke out a living in a foreign country. This seems to be a sound decision under the circumstances, though sojourning is not without its risks. To have remained as 1:3 indicates is simply due to the ongoing famine. When Elimelech dies, Naomi and her two sons seem destined to stay in Moab. The sons take Moabite wives, Orpah and Ruth, making the family even more trapped in Moab. If things weren't bad enough, Naomi's sons both die after living there 10 years. Not only that, they both failed to produce children. For Naomi, a Jewish woman living under the mandate of raising children to fear God, this would have been tragic indeed. She is left with no one to carry on her husband's inheritance. Even half Moabite children would have been better than none!

Stuck in Moab
To be in "exile" in Moab would be bitter largely because of its history. In Genesis 19:34-38 the daughters of Lot express the primal yearning for offspring. They have just survived the destruction of Sodom and are hiding in a cave with their father. They don't know the status of their fellow man and assume the worst: that all other people have been destroyed. In desperation they trick their father into getting drunk and they each take turns sleeping with him "to preserve offspring from their father." As a result the oldest daughter bore a son named Moab, father of the Moabites and the younger also bore a son named Ben-ammi, the father of the Ammonites. Ironically, the country of Moab doesn't prove to be a fertile place for Elimelech's family. Naomi seems to be worse off now than when they fled to Moab.

It is in 1:6 that Naomi dared to dream of returning to her homeland. "She had heard in the fields of Moab that the Lord had visited his people and given them food." These "whispers of grace" could be compared to the witness of Christian believers who talk freely of Jesus. Our God centered perspective can have a vital impact on the decisions of others. Naomi was hearing rumors of hope from others in the field. This meant to Naomi that it was time to go home. Even without husband and sons, she would get back to Bethlehem. Where else do you go when all else has failed? No one wants to return empty handed, but home is the place where they have to let you in! So Naomi arises from her mourning and heads off for Bethlehem. This journey takes a measure of faith and courage. It seems that Orpah and Ruth are drawn to travel with Naomi.

The Hand of The Lord
Orpah and Ruth are childless widows in a bad predicament. They are not of the same faith as Naomi, but they see her faith and are drawn by it. Based on 1:6-14 it is evident that both the young women are devoted to their mother-in-law. But something stops Naomi from allowing her daughters-in-law to continue on the journey. She doesn't want them to sacrifice their lives for her. There is the Hebrew custom (Deut. 25:5-10) of levirate marriage in which the brother or nearest male relative of a childless, deceased man is to marry his widow and produce children and heirs for his bloodline. Naomi and her daughters-in-law are certainly familiar with this custom. Naomi is either too distressed to remember, or simply does not know of any such kinsmen in Elimelech's family. She is not sure what she will find in Bethlehem. Maybe she is not even sure if her property remains intact. The blessing she gives the girls in verse eight is suggestive of their mutual respect and affection: "The Lord grant that you may find rest, each of you in the house of her husband!" She also indicates that they have been kind to their husbands and to her. Naomi is a mature woman with noble motives. She wants what is best for Orpah and Ruth: remarriage and children. To these women of ancient times marriage and family was the prescription for rest. Rest defined as a state of calm and refreshment. Maybe we would call it completion or fulfillment. To our regrettable post modern way of thinking rest isn't even the goal.

They refuse to go back. With much weeping they cry, "No, we will return with you to your people." But they don't fully understand the problem. Naomi, the older and wiser woman does. She uses an analogy to show them the futility of accompanying her. Just as it would be impossible for her to birth more sons for them to marry, she has nothing to offer. She can't promise them any prospects for remarriage. The absurdity of wasting her life on this venture must have hit home to Orpah.

Naomi explains that "the hand of the Lord has gone out against me." And this is true. One of the hardest things for believers to stomach is the realization that God's treatment of us is not something we can control by being good or faithful. His decisions and actions are not always or even mostly about us. He is sovereign in good and bad times. Naomi does not try to "candy coat" her sovereign God by blaming circumstances on any other person or thing. She is sorry for her daughters, but sees all of her difficulties as coming from God and warns them of the hazards of going back to Bethlehem.

I believe there is an oft overlooked element of realism in Naomi's faith. A realism that is very foreign to popular Christian thinking. It takes humility and faith to see God as sovereign over everything. Even if it can't be packaged neatly for evangelism purposes, it is more honest and biblical than we are used to hearing. This kind of God centered faith, though grief laden, seems to have grabbed Ruth by the heart and laid hold on her. Through Naomi's gritty, determined faith and witness, Ruth has been exposed to the Holy One of Israel. No false God of the Moabites could compare to the greatness and mercy of Naomi's God. When Naomi says to Ruth in 1:15, "See, your sister-in-law has gone back to her people and to her gods; return after your sister-in-law," Ruth gives a beautiful and revered response used in wedding ceremonies to this day.

Ruth's Confession
With these words in 1:16-17 Ruth confesses her faith in Naomi's God and devotion to her: "Do not urge me to leave you or to return from following you. For where you go I will go, and where you lodge I will lodge. Your people shall be my people, and your God my God. Where you die I will die, and there will I be buried. May the Lord do so to me and more also if anything but death parts me from you." In other words, somewhere along the dusty road from Moab to Bethlehem, Ruth has expanded her vision. She has become more than just loyal to Naomi. Her heart has been changed. She has come to know and embrace Naomi's God. Because of this godly and intentional determination on Ruth's part, Naomi allows her to remain with her.

Naomi's Testimony

Naomi and Ruth cause quite a stir when they arrive in Bethlehem. In 1:19 the women of the town exclaim, "Is this Naomi?" Not a flattering welcome home! I don't imagine the two women would have looked their best after a long journey possibly on foot. Nor would Naomi have been easily recognized as she approached the town without her husband and sons.

The weary and grieving woman answers the direct concern of her neighbors with a very sad, but honest testimonial: "Do not call me Naomi [pleasant]; call me Mara [bitter], for the Almighty has dealt very bitterly with me. I went away full, and the Lord has brought me back empty. Why call me Naomi, when the Lord has testified against me and the Almighty has brought calamity upon me?" Here's how I would paraphrase it as if Naomi had just gotten off a Greyhound bus and walked with her suitcase and daughter-in-law all the way to my church just in time for the worship service. "I may resemble that young woman you used to know named Naomi, for 'pleasant.' That's what I was when I left here many years ago with high hopes and a family. But I return to you now with no husband, and no sons. The Lord has seen fit to deal with me bitterly, so call me 'bitter.' I don't understand it, but God has brought tragedy upon me."

If Naomi were to walk into one of our women's Bible studies in today's culture with these sad words, what might be our response? We would probably rush to correct her and assure her that the tragedies of her life do not come from God. Maybe some would say she was suffering the consequences of bad judgment on the part of her husband. Or some might try to comfort her with assurances that the calamities of her life are attacks from Satan. Certainly, the present day mindset is so limited by man-centered theology that even many Christians don't see the pain and suffering of life as coming from the hand of God! Maybe He has allowed it, but certainly not ordained it! Hmm….

Naomi was not like us. She had more in common with Job who gave God his due when he received news of his children's deaths. He said in Job 1:21 "The Lord giveth, and the Lord taketh away; blessed be the name of the Lord." Naomi shared the view of Joseph, who understood that when his brothers sold him into slavery, God was behind it all. He said, "It was not you who sent me here, but God" in Genesis 45:8. Their high view of God's sovereignty gave them a vantage point during times of trial.

Throughout Scripture, God's people understand that calamities, attacks, illnesses, and so forth, all ultimately come from His sovereign hand. Many unbelievers see our faith as weak and shallow when we can't reconcile the power and seemingly juxtaposed compassion of our God. We want others to perceive Him as nice and fair by earthly standards. We want people to be won over by our "good press" for God. Well, maybe He would rather people, including his children, be in awe of his power. Naomi's faith was not about making God out to be some nice guy who is always fair and waits for people to choose the right thing. She didn't make the journey back to Bethlehem for a God who has his hands tied by human events. I believe Naomi, and Ruth, went back to Bethlehem to be with people who understood that regardless of circumstances God is to be worshipped, obeyed, and followed because He is worthy! They were compelled by a force that could not be summarized in neatly packaged sound bites. Naomi's faith has a touch of grit and disillusionment which makes her authentic. She is holding on to God in a way that inspires us to leave behind the man-centered theology of today. When the two women arrive they aren't looking for an escape or positive spin. They show up in time for barley harvest. There is work to be done.

Gleaning

Unbeknownst to Naomi and Ruth, God has provided a kinsman redeemer. Things are not quite as horrible as Naomi assumed in her grief stricken condition. As a sort of explanation to the reader, Ruth 2:1 tells us that Naomi has a relative by marriage named Boaz who is a "worthy man." This clansman of Elimelech's is well known to his community, but not yet part of Naomi's thinking.

Later in verse three there is a hint that Boaz is back in Bethlehem getting filled in on the story and reputation of Ruth who has already been recognized by others for her kindness to Naomi. The unknown author of Ruth has set the stage for us to see the energy and initiative of Ruth. She asks Naomi to let her go to the barley fields and glean some of the grain that is purposely dropped by the reapers for the poor—and indeed they are poor. Whatever they owned back in Moab was either meager or sold for food. They probably arrived with nothing. So Ruth has assessed the situation with a practical look toward the future. She will go where the hard working poor go and hope for reapers to be favorable.

Does the combination of daring and humility on Ruth's part sink in? How would you feel about asking the workers in a restaurant if you could take home the scraps of food to be thrown away in exchange for scrubbing and cleaning? As a woman in a foreign country, which was coming out of a famine, Ruth had to throw herself at the mercy of people she didn't know and who weren't much better off than she. Instead of getting depressed or polarized by disappointment, Ruth got busy. She willingly took on the role of provider for Naomi. Perhaps they could stay in a safe place in Bethlehem, but food was scarce for everyone. So, off to the fields Ruth went. In 2:6-7 we are told that the foreman of the reapers noticed that Ruth worked inexhaustibly.

Ruth was immediately noticed by Boaz, in whose field she was unknowingly gleaning. When he returns from Bethlehem (obviously the farming is done outside of the city) Boaz greets his reapers with the words, "The Lord be with you!" They answer him with, "The Lord bless you." Then Boaz asks his foreman about the woman he does not recognize. According to the servant/foreman who was in charge of the reapers, Ruth is known for two things: her loyalty to Naomi and her hard work.

Treated Like A Lady

In 2:8-9 Boaz then speaks to Ruth with compassion: In summary he calls her daughter, a term of protectiveness; kindly commands her to stay in his fields with his women reapers; assures her that his young men have been told to leave her alone; and to drink the water drawn by his young men. In verse 10 we see that these words have a powerful effect on Ruth who falls to her face, bowing on the ground.

In astonishment Ruth exclaims in 2:10, "Why have I found favor in your eyes, that you should take notice of me, since I am a foreigner?" I don't think we can say enough about Boaz going out of his way for Ruth. Her response indicates more than mere politeness or modesty. She is blown away. She is on her face and bowed to the ground when she marvels at his kindness. Why should this man, known for his worthiness, and the owner of the field in which she is doing the lowly work of gleaning, even notice her, much less protect her?

His answer in 2:11-13 is simply that he has heard all about her while in Bethlehem. Boaz knows Ruth is a widow. He knows she has left her parents and native land to come to a strange place. His foreman has told him about her willingness to work extremely hard—and the people of Bethlehem have told him about her willingness to sacrifice for her mother-in-law. Boaz blesses Ruth with these beautiful words: "The Lord repay you for what you have done, and a full reward be given you by the Lord, the God of Israel, under whose wings you have come to take refuge!" (Ruth 2:12)

What stands out most to me in all that Boaz says is that Ruth's behavior is seen as an act of faith in God. Yes, she loves her mother-in-law, but she has put her faith in God! There is something about Ruth's faith and loyalty which appeals to Boaz. We are told nothing about Ruth's physical appearance. It is her character which stands out to Boaz.

Later at mealtime, in 2:14, Boaz invites Ruth to share the meal with him and his reapers. He passes Ruth the grain and she eats her fill with some left over. Boaz also instructs his young men, saying, "Let her glean even among the sheaves, and do not reproach her. And also pull out some of the bundles for her and leave it for her to glean, and do not rebuke her." I believe Ruth's reputation and demeanor inspired Boaz to treat her like a lady. He could have seen her competence as an excuse to leave her to her own devices. Instead, he behaves like a protector, or rescuer. Much like our Savior, Boaz surprises Ruth with his compassion and generosity.

The Redeemer
Earlier when Naomi began her journey back to Bethlehem we had a picture of salvation. Here we have another picture of Christ's redeeming love for His bride, the Church, when Boaz provides Ruth with protection and favor. His compassion is always a surprise to repentant sinners.

So Ruth worked until evening and took her gleanings into the city to her mother-in-law. She showed the barley to Naomi and gave her the left over food she had saved. When Naomi hears from Ruth that the man who has shown favor to her is Boaz, she takes comfort in knowing that he is one of her relatives, or redeemers. In 2:22 the wise woman tells Ruth to "stay with Boaz's young women, lest you be assaulted." Ruth listened to and lived with her mother-in-law in Bethlehem, far from the barley fields.

Naomi's Intuition
We know from the preceding events that much of Boaz's knowledge about Ruth came from what people said about her. The people in town had spread the word of her arrival with Naomi, and Boaz had relied on information from his foreman to learn more of her character. Now we learn in 3:1 that Naomi has a sense about a need within Ruth that could be fulfilled by Boaz. It wouldn't be hard for her to know that marriage would be nice for her young daughter-in-law. Hopefully it's not too speculative to assume that Naomi's intuition was from hearing things about Boaz from other people. Could there have been talk about him being smitten with Ruth? Certainly his attention to Ruth's safety and welfare would have been noticed by others. Would the existence of another

kinsman redeemer (mentioned in 3:12) and a great age difference have been enough to discourage Boaz from pursuing Ruth as a wife? I think the text suggests in 2:23—3:2 that the ingredients for romance are gathered, Naomi sees it, and Boaz is timid.

After many weeks of Ruth working in the fields all day long with Boaz's young women, Naomi reveals her plan to Ruth in 3:1-4: "My daughter, should I not seek rest for you that it may be well with you? Is not Boaz our relative, with whose young women you were? See, he is winnowing barley tonight at the threshing floor. Wash therefore and anoint yourself, and put on your cloak and go down to the threshing floor, but do not make yourself known to the man until he has finished eating and drinking. But when he lies down, observe the place where he lies. Then go and uncover his feet and lie down, and he will tell you what to do." Notice that at the end of verse 4 Naomi credits Boaz with the wisdom and leadership to be trustworthy.

Naomi's Vision
Naomi is simply showing Ruth how to act in a way that is overlooked in today's world: taking the initiative to invite a man to lead. After all, she can probably see that the two care for each other. So she gives practical advice to Ruth to catch her man in a way that will encourage his leadership!

Notice that one of the sensible things Naomi tells Ruth to do is get cleaned up and pretty! One of my grandmothers use to say, "Always make sure you look good whenever you have something important to do. A woman who takes time with her appearance will never regret it." To some this may seem glaringly obvious. To others this may seem like outmoded advice. I suspect that Naomi wanted to make sure that her daughter-in-law who was working in the fields everyday still knew how to be a lady. Older generations who grew up with more tradition and formality tend to be more observant about these things. We should listen to them. Fortunately Ruth was very teachable.

So, verses 6-13 tell the way Ruth reveals her heart to Boaz.

After working hard, and celebrating the harvest with his workers, Boaz sleeps at the end of his heap of grain, presumably to protect it from thieves and avoid the journey home late at night. Ruth, wearing the cloak Naomi told her to wear, tip-toes in, uncovers his feet (or perhaps literally uncovers him), and lies down until he wakes up. Astonished to find a woman at his feet, Boaz exclaims, "Who are you?" Ruth then speaks in her own words, not Naomi's: "I am Ruth, your servant. Spread your wings over your servant, for you are a redeemer."

What was Ruth thinking when she said this? These are her words not Naomi's. Did she plan out her response based on some custom or ritual? On the contrary, chapter 2:12 indicates a precedent set by Boaz for her choice of words. Earlier when Boaz saw the faith and character of Ruth he blessed her with these words: "The Lord repay you for what you have done, and a full reward be given you by the Lord, the God of Israel, under whose wings you have come to take refuge!" I believe Ruth's words were in response to the initial understanding and compassion of Boaz. When they first met he understood her. He didn't see her as someone to be pitied. He didn't try to take advantage of her or allow others to. He saw God working in her and told her so! He let her know how her qualities affected him! These are powerful things to any woman.

Though chaste, Ruth's words and actions on the threshing floor that night had a seductive effect on Boaz. Now that this young woman has told him that she wants his God and she wants him too, Boaz knows where he stands with her. In 3:10 he refers to her kind attention and affection as a kindness even greater than her first of being loyal to Naomi: "You have made this last kindness greater than the first in that you have not gone after young men, whether poor or rich." In the midst of all this romantic declaration, Boaz demonstrates great level-headedness and self-control. He won't rush into anything. He wants to do things properly. I doubt if he laid a hand on her.

Protective of Ruth's reputation (which he describes as that of a "worthy woman" in 3:11), Boaz promises that he will do what she has asked. But he is thorough in his approach. He will go directly to the one possible obstacle. In 3:13 a reference to the other redeemer implies that Boaz is willing to yield to God's will in the matter.

Ruth remains at Boaz's feet until morning, arises before anyone could recognize her, and when he sends her off he warns others not to speak of the presence of a woman on the threshing floor. And he also measures out six measures of barley for her to take into the city for her mother-in-law. Boaz is circumspect about Ruth's reputation and thoughtful of Naomi, knowing that she depends on Ruth for every morsel of food.

Encouragement From Naomi
When Naomi saw Ruth coming toward the city gate that morning what do you suppose she found? I speculate that Ruth might have been a bit apprehensive. Perhaps the reference to the other, closer kinsman redeemer would seem like a great obstacle. It is not necessarily reassuring to know that the man you want to marry wants God's will first in the matter. Naomi's words in 3:18 seem designed to buoy up the younger woman's confidence: "Wait, my daughter, until you learn how the matter turns out, for the man will not rest but will settle the matter today." So, perhaps while the two women lingered nearby, Boaz took his place at the city gate and got to work on the problem. Once again, Naomi encourages Ruth to trust the leadership of Boaz. It is inspiring to see the assertive steps the man takes to keep his promises.

Boaz the Redeemer
In Ruth 4 we have the account of Boaz assertively approaching the other kinsman. When speaking to Ruth earlier, Boaz seemed confident that he could take care of Ruth's problem. The trick is in understanding her problem. It is not that she is madly in love with Boaz and wants to be his wife, however true that may be. Ruth's difficulty is that she is a widow, her mother-in-law is a widow, and

there are no children to inherit from the line of Elimelech. Unless she were to remarry a kinsman redeemer who could provide her with children after purchasing their inheritance from them, she is destined to fail in her mission as a Jewish woman. Property was meant to be passed on to children, not just accumulated by widows. Understand that apart from choosing to be a Jewish woman who would follow Namoi's God and live with her, Ruth was free to remarry anyone she chose. To have committed to God and Naomi complicates things for Ruth. Or rather, simplifies things in that she now has only two choices: Boaz or the other unnamed kinsman. Clearly, no matter how Boaz feels about Ruth, he sees the problem in terms of redeeming the blood line of Elimelech, which could be solved by marrying either of the two men. Naomi, Ruth, and Boaz are trusting God in a big way. They have certain desires and dreams. But with spiritual clarity, their greatest desire is to follow God's will. This is a thing called faithfulness. In summary all of this makes the faithfulness of Ruth even more remarkable than what would be reasonable to expect.

    Boaz sat down at the city gate and waited for the kinsman-redeemer to show up. When he does come by Boaz invites him to sit down for a chat. Then Boaz tells ten of the city elders to sit down with them. Notice the succinct way in which Boaz tells the other man the story of Naomi's plight. In verses 3-5 the situation is presented in a way that would most appeal to the redeemer. Not until the man indicates his desire to acquire the parcel of land does Boaz tell him about Ruth. This suggests to me that Boaz wants to be honest in his portrayal of the situation. He doesn't believe that he deserves to be cut any slack. Then when Boaz makes clear to the redeemer that this right of redemption also includes Ruth he declines the offer. My guess is that this man is a widower with children whose own inheritance he does not wish to dilute. Or perhaps he has a wife.

    In verse 8 the customary transaction takes place right there at the city gate for all to see. The sandals of the kinsmen are exchanged. In verse 10 Boaz declares to all the people: "I have acquired Ruth to be my wife, to perpetuate the name of the dead in his inheritance that the name of the dead may not be cut off from among his brothers and from the gate of his native place. You are witnesses this day." The text implies in 3:18 and 4:9 that Ruth and Naomi must have been standing nearby during all this. In 4:11 the people and elders said, "We are witnesses. May the Lord make the woman, who is coming into your house, like Rachel and Leah, who together built up the house of Israel...." These people don't mess around with euphemisms. They want the couple to reproduce! This would be the whole point of marriage from the perspective of faithful Hebrews. God put this compulsion in Adam and Eve. He commanded it to Noah's sons. He prophesied it to Abraham. He showed his blessing by the prolific numbers of his chosen people. The blessing of the Bethlehemites reflected the passion of God. That His people would one day bring forth the Messiah. Sure there would have been exceptions for some couples then as now concerning the success of bringing children into the world. But the vision for marriage would have been that a man and woman would "teach their children God's laws, so the next generation would know them, even the children yet to be born, and they in turn would tell their children. Then they would put their trust in God and would not forget his deeds but would keep his commands." (Ps.78:5b-7)

Naomi's Fulfillment
In Ruth 4:13-17 is one of Scripture's most poignant accounts of God's sovereign grace. Boaz takes Ruth as his wife, they conceive and bear a son. The women in this community see this as a blessing for Naomi, "Blessed be the Lord, who has not left you this day without a redeemer, and may his name be renowned in Israel..." A careful reading of this would indicate that the redeemer of whom they speak is not Boaz, but Boaz's son. The fact that this child has been birthed by Ruth, who is "worth more than seven sons" is the praiseworthy quality given to him. (4:15) Naomi then takes the child onto her lap and cares for him. I think she lived in the home

with Boaz and Ruth. I think she found her complete joy in caring for her grandchild. Truly her faithfulness to God is rewarded. Imagine the excitement of Naomi's friends who exclaimed as they visited the new baby, "A son has been born to Naomi." They named him Obed. The story of Naomi and Ruth and Boaz had touched their community deeply. The child seems to be celebrated and loved by all. How appropriate since the child they named Obed would become the grandfather of King David!

The book of Ruth is really about Naomi. It is as if in God's cosmic production Ruth was willing to play a supporting role to her distressed mother-in-law. She was compelled by the grace of God to support and follow Naomi to Bethlehem, a place of famine. She was intrigued by Naomi's faith and willing to forsake personal security. Naomi journeyed back to her home of Bethlehem without knowing that God had a kinsman waiting for her. She couldn't see or understand God's plan at the time, but she trusted his sovereign power.

Most importantly, Ruth was brought into the family of faith shared by Naomi and her people. How could she have known that her actions would inspire a worthy man, Boaz, to love and admire her? How could she or Naomi have known that their mourning and destitution in Moab would result in vindication back in Bethlehem? Who would have thought that anything good could come out of Moab—especially the line of David?

Womanly Discipleship
Where would Naomi and Ruth have been without each other? They would have been like many of us in today's world of personal isolation. Today a "Naomi" could only dream of a respectful daughter-in-law. And even if there are Ruth's out there, many older women have long forgotten those maternal instincts which used to be directed toward young women and their children. As far as I am concerned, Naomi is the hero because she nurtured Ruth. She had an edgy, real, and God centered faith which inspired Ruth to follow. God's grace was working in Ruth and she responded with

faith. Why else would a young woman leave her native land and culture? Orpah wanted to follow, but she was not strong enough. Naomi didn't just want company on the journey. She needed a disciple with back bone, which was amply demonstrated by Ruth. We younger women have an example in Ruth of a vibrant, strong, loyal, and teachable woman. Older women who have experienced joys and defeat have an example in Naomi of a woman who is honest but hopeful, strong but able to accept help.

We, like Naomi and Ruth, are daily faced with decisive moments of faithfulness to God. When questions and challenges arise, we may fail to see God at the center of everything. Never underestimate his power or goodness. When your world is falling apart, be a Naomi and return to your origins of faith. Take along a trusted Ruth and cling to the many promises in Scripture like Paul's in Romans 8:28, "We know that in all things God works for the good of those who love him, who have been called according to his purpose."

Questions for Study and Discussion:

1. Naomi is a woman with many difficulties. Based on Ruth 1:5, what is her main dilemma?

2. Before answering the following questions carefully read Ruth 1:19-22.

   What might have caused Naomi's people to be so stirred by her return?

   What does Naomi's response tell us about her personality and her faith?

   Is this the way a Christian woman should view the calamities and disappointments of life?

3. Chapter tells us a lot about the character and personality of Boaz. Make a list of the characteristics described or hinted at from the time Boaz enters the scene until 2:23.

4. Ruth also gives a lot about Ruth's character. Please list characteristics of Ruth that would have been relevant to the others around her.

5. Boaz, the kinsman redeemer, has been compared to Jesus, the Savior. How would you compare the two in terms of behavior in Ruth ? Please point to specific verses when giving examples.

6. In Ruth 3:1-6, Naomi gives practical advice to Ruth concerning Boaz. Make a list of each thing with its possible purpose.

7. Did you notice that the nature of the list is not comprehensive? What does this suggest about their mother/daughter relationship?

8. Based on Ruth 2:20-22; 3:1-4, and 3:18, do you agree with

the author of this study that Naomi encourages Ruth to trust Boaz's leadership? Please give specific answers.

9. How was Naomi's emptiness filled?

10. Ruth 4:16 is the true resolution of Naomi's conflict. Is there still a place in our society for believers to have the kind of unity and interaction seen in Ruth?

11. In Matthew 1:1-17 we are given the geneology of Jesus Christ.

    Who from this study is present in the bloodline of Jesus?

    Who was Boaz' mother?

    How might this relate to his choice of wife?

12. Ruth 1:16-17 is Ruth's declaration of loyalty to Naomi. These verses are often recited at weddings. Why?

5

DEBORAH: A WOMAN OF VICTORY

Scripture References:
Judges 4—5
1 Samuel 12:11—Barak listed as one of the deliverers sent by God to Israel
Hebrews 11:32—Barak listed in Hall of Faith

Judges 1-3

The book of Judges is set in the tumultuous time (1380-1050 B.C.) of Israel's efforts to complete the occupation of the Promised Land. Led into the land by Joshua, Moses' successor, the people of God were commanded to drive out the pagan inhabitants of Canaan. The people did not obey the Lord's instruction regarding this after Joshua died. Joshua 2:10-11 takes the pulse of the nation after the death of Joshua, "And all that generation also were gathered to their fathers. And there arose another generation after them who did not know the Lord or the work that he had done for Israel. And the people of Israel did what was evil in the sight of the Lord and served the Baals."

Some of the tribes of Israel made failed attempts to drive out the pagans. Others put the Canaanites to forced labor (1:28) but did not truly obey God by driving them out. This partial obedience and compromise led to the corruption of Israel. They lost sight of God and his mighty works. They intermarried. They allowed the pagan religion of Baal to commingle with Judaism. Baal was the god of rain and fertility. Ashtoreths were the female consorts of Baal. The worship of Baal and his other false gods and goddesses included animal sacrifices, male and female prostitution, and sometimes human sacrifices.

When Joshua first led the people in, they experienced relative victory. They defeated the enemy armies. They inhabited the new territories. But they failed to live up to God's standard of absolute obedience. The conquest was not completed on God's terms. They took the easy way out many times over.

Then the Lord raised up judges. Yet they did not listen to them for "they whored after other gods and bowed down to them." (2:17) So there continued a repetitive cycle of idol worship, punishment, repentance, deliverance, idol worship, punishment, repentance, …. By allowing their children to intermarry, Baal worship flourished. Interestingly, it was always God's people who got corrupted and weakened, not the pagans. This would allow their enemies to gain a stronghold, conquer and oppress them, thereby forcing them to cry out to God. Repeatedly God would send a judge to lead the people and deliver them from the Ammonites, the Hittites, the Perizzites, the Moabites, and the Canaanites. God became alternately angry at the faithlessness of his people, letting them experience punishment at the hands of their enemies; and alternately merciful in sending a deliverer. The first deliverer/judge was Othniel. The Spirit of the Lord was with him and the land had rest forty years. Then the people of Israel got into trouble again and the Lord sent them another deliverer named Ehud. The Spirit of the Lord was with him and the land had rest for eighty years.

Once again, in chapter 4 the people of Israel did what was evil in the sight of the Lord after Ehud died. The Lord sold them into the hand of Jabin King of Canaan. The commander of his army was Sisera, who oppressed the people cruelly for twenty years.

It may come as a surprise for post moderns to see that the Bible explicitly teaches that God does punish sin and sinners. He especially punishes Israel because he holds his people to the highest of standards. He was angry with Israel, but he had promised to keep them in covenant with him so that he could demonstrate his mercy. Often when God gives us a second chance, or break, it's not about our deserving it. It's about his desire to be glorified!

Accordingly, God sends his next deliverer: Deborah, a prophetess, the wife of Lappidoth, and judge of Israel at that time. The two things about Deborah that are crucial to understand are from Judges 4:4-6: "Now Deborah, a prophetess, the wife of Lappidoth, was judging Israel at that time. She used to sit under the palm of Deborah between Ramah and Bethel in the hill country of Ephraim, and the people of Israel came up to her for judgment." First, the name of Deborah's husband is given for a reason. The male judge's wives are not named. So why do we need to know who Deborah is married to? Especially since he is never referred to again. I think it is so that we will know that she has a life apart from her ministry as prophetess and judge. Like all godly wives, her first ministry is to her husband. She serves God faithfully and with excellence. Nevertheless she serves under the authority of her husband and his support. There is no mention of children. This suggests that if Deborah has children they are grown, hence the increased likelihood of wisdom!

The second thing is the way in which Deborah carries out her ministry. People come to her under a tree in her back yard. She does not have to be away from home to reach people. She holds court, so to speak, by taking callers and hearing their cases one by one on her own turf. I believe this style of ministry reflects a godly commitment on Deborah's part to be a woman for her family first. Her ministry is incorporated into her life. Not visa versa. She possibly has her husband nearby and is not using her gifts in a way that could jeopardize her marriage.

Along with all of this is the simple fact that Deborah stands out as a compelling woman. She can wait for people to come to her because God leads them to her. She lives in the presence of God and has a faith and personality reflective of that. When Deborah advises Barak, she does so as a woman of uncommon clarity. This has a forceful effect in a sinful and corrupt society.

The stage has been set for us to see Deborah as empowered by God to minister in some capacity, though limited by the fact of her gender. Also, we are able to see that her ministry is effective enough to compel others to come to her.

In 4:6-10 Deborah sends for Barak, another judge and the military leader of the Israelites. Because of the words of Deborah to Barak, it would seem that Barak is avoiding God:

"She sent and summoned Barak the son of Abinoam from Kedesh-naphtali and said to him, "Has not the Lord, the God of Israel, commanded you, 'Go, gather your men at Mount Tabor, taking ten thousand men from the people of Naphtali and the people of Zebulun. And I will draw out Sisera, the general of Jabin's army, to meet you by the river Kishon with his chariots and his troops, and I will give him into your hand.'" Barak said to her, "If you will go with me, I will go, but if you will not go with me, I will not go." And she said, "I will surely go with you. Nevertheless, the road on which you are going will not lead to your glory, for the Lord will sell Sisera into the hand of a woman." Then Deborah arose and went with Barak to Kedesh. And Barak called out Zebulun and Naphtali to Kadesh. And ten thousand men went up at his heels, and Deborah went up with him."

Here are important observations from the text above found in Judges 4:4-10.

1. Deborah had to send for Barak.

2. He knew the prophecy and wasn't already obeying God.

3. By questioning him she held him accountable for being passive.

4. Her words were correct.

5. Barak is weak in his resolve without Deborah, "If you will go with me, I will go…"

6. Deborah agrees to go.

7. She warns him of further prophecy about a woman completing his mission.

8. Deborah goes with Barak and stays with him to complete victory.

Deborah is a woman of faith and obedience. The two are inexorably linked. Barak is a man of faith as well. But when he becomes afraid to do the difficult thing God commands, instead of taking steps to obey he hesitates. Hesitating, or hiding, is the same thing as disobeying. I believe that God wanted Deborah to know Barak's orders so that she could hold him accountable and encourage him. In the kingdom of God, a leader's orders from God are usually public. It is a matter of concern to everyone when a leader fails to obey God to the fullest.

Truth +Faith= Wisdom
Have you ever doubted the truth or hesitated to do the right thing until someone comes along and reminds you of it? As a prophet, Deborah is very in touch with the truth and a clear sense of right and wrong—and totally trusts in God. She knows he can be counted on and is worthy of obedience. Put the two together and you have WISDOM. James 1:5-8 gives a prescription for godly wisdom: "If any of you lacks wisdom, let him ask God, who gives generously to all without reproach, and it will be given him. But let him ask in faith, with no doubting, for the one who doubts is like a wave of the sea that is driven and tossed by the wind. For that person must not suppose that he will receive anything from the Lord; he is a double minded man, unstable in all his ways."

There is nothing double minded about Deborah.

As a woman with biblical clarity there is something very crucial here that Deborah grasps which would behoove us to understand in today's world. Deborah knows very deep in her soul that her people need Barak. She has a vision for masculine leadership. Yet she is a woman! Today we women need to appreciate what God created men to do and be as masculine leaders. Their leadership is not optional or expendable. We women cannot somehow replace men or feminize leadership to fit our gifts or perspectives. If we want to be like Deborah who was a gifted leader in her own right, we must start with understanding that God has ordained the primary leadership of his church, like the nation of Israel, to be led by men. When men do not rise to this challenge it hurts women. When women interfere with masculinity it hurts men and women. Deborah is able to see the circumstances of Barak's challenges and encourage him without ruining him as a leader.

Barak is weak in his resolve. His intentions are good, he wants to do the right thing, but he is overwhelmed. He lacks the courage of his convictions. And it's no surprise if you look at his environment. Israel is once again beaten down by a tyrant. Her people are caught up in moral corruption which has made them prey to oppressors. Barak and his generation are even worse off than those who lived when Joshua died "who did not know the Lord or the work that he had done for Israel" in 2:10. Who knows the depth of depravity to which the people have fallen? Who knows if he has any true comrades in which to trust? We do know from 4:3 that Sisera had nine hundred chariots of iron. The Canaanites' were the most advanced and powerful of their time. To put it simply, Barak needs inspiration and support. He needs Deborah.

The Road to Glory
Deborah is supportive but does not coddle Barak. In Judges 4:6-9, we have what is probably a condensed version of her conversation with Barak. In the course of what may have been a lengthy discussion in an effort to embolden Barak, precious time is dwindling. Every minute wasted could cost them the battle. God must have told her how the Canaanite general would be slain. She warns him that even though he must pull up the boot straps, there will be personal consequences for not responding

to God quickly. In 4:9 Deborah says to Barak, "I will surely go with you. Nevertheless, the road on which you are going will not lead to your glory, for the Lord will sell Sisera into the hand of a woman." What is the bottom line in what Deborah says to Barak? Why should Barak care about his glory? There are important implications here to explore.

Throughout scripture God makes it clear that his glory and demonstrating his glory is of the utmost importance to him. His glory, plainly put, is the sum of his great attributes. When the Lord decides to display His glorious sovereign power, His mercy, His might, His holiness, His patience, His wisdom, etc...no obstacle can hinder Him. No earthly or heavenly being can thwart His plans. As Isaiah 40:5 says, "And the glory of the Lord shall be revealed, and all flesh shall see it together, for the mouth of the Lord has spoken." God reveals His glory in many small ways throughout history, and promises a future time of revealing His full glory. This is not at stake because of anyone's disobedience.

Since God's own glory is not at stake, Barak's refusal to obey the commands of God without Deborah's backing is going to suppress instead of elucidate that glory in his own life. His immediate responsibility is to gather an army from the people of Naphtali and the people of Zebulon numbering ten thousand and meet at Mount Tabor. Then God promises to draw Sisera into battle so that they can fight against his chariots and troops. No amount of human bravery would relish such a prospect. Even if Barak believes that God can help them overcome the odds, he's got to convince the people of God. He probably doubts his own ability to enlist ten thousand men. Deborah is a respected and wise judge. Surely her presence will lend credibility to the mission. Surely the people of God will follow him if Deborah goes up with him to call together troops.

We don't know how much time Deborah had to spend persuading Barak. Judges 4:6-8 could well be a condensed version of their discussions. Is Deborah alluding to a dangerous waste of time, when time is of the essence in battle? Perhaps her prophetic warning that Barak's enemy will be given over to a woman is largely due to Barak's hesitance which will keep him from intercepting Cisera before he escapes to friendly quarters. At any rate, it is a disgrace for a warrior, especially a general, to miss the opportunity to personally destroy his enemy, but an even greater dishonor for the privilege to go to a woman.

As a consequence for his fear, Barak is in a terrible position of knowing that he must remain faithful to God without the privilege of sharing in the glory by demonstrating total trust in God. There is still satisfaction in obeying and the consequential relief from judgment. There is still the fact that Barak can fight for his people. There is still the chance for him to not fail God. But Deborah warns him that if he insists on her going with him that God will withhold from him the one thing that a great warrior wants and that God specifically promised: the honor of personally slaying the horrible enemy, Sisera (as mentioned in 4:7). By not acting quickly enough, Barak forfeits this promise and the special glory that God would have manifested in his chosen leader's vindication.

This Is The Day!
We are told that Deborah goes with Barak to Kadesh where he gathers ten thousand fighting men. I think he was afraid and believed that her presence would better ensure victory. It has already been noted that people come to Deborah for her wisdom. Deborah is not a warrior, but Barak insists that she prop him up. She accompanies Barak and his men up to Mount Tabor. When Sisera hears that Barak has assembled at Mount Tabor, he calls out his troops and 900 chariots of iron. It seems in verse 14 that Deborah is still propping up Barak. She tells him, "Up! For this is the day in which the Lord has given Sisera into your hand. Does not the Lord go out before you?"

So Barak rises to the occasion and defeats Sisera. According to 4:16 Barak pursues the chariots and the army to the home town of Sisera, defeating all the army of Sisera, leaving not one man alive. Despite his earlier reluctance, he demonstrates great bravery in his defeat of Sisera.

The Hand of a Woman
Sisera the tormentor has now become a pathetic coward fleeing Barak on foot. He runs to the tent of Jael whose husband's family is friendly to the Canaanite king Jaban. Jael comes out to meet Sisera and persuades him not to be afraid, but to come into her tent. Jael demonstrates quick wit. She covers the frightened and shivering man with a blanket. Then, to quench his thirst, she gives him milk, even though he only asked for water. She makes sure he is comfortable and warm with the blanket and agrees to stand at the opening of the tent to make sure no one finds him sleeping there.

Jael is a very brave and resourceful woman. She also knows which side of the battle she is on. She doesn't hesitate or cringe from doing something hard. While Sisera sleeps without any tinge of conscience, Jael picks up the tools familiar to tent dwelling women of her day, and drives the tent peg into Sisera's temple. She literally nails the man's head to the ground. In fulfillment of Deborah's prophecy, Jael greets Barak as he is coming towards her tent in pursuit of Sisera and says to him, "'Come, and I will show you the man whom you are seeking.' So he went in to her tent, and there laid Sisera dead, with the tent peg in his temple."

Jael could have been timid about luring Sisera into her tent. She might have been in doubt as to her role once he was there alone with her, but instead she had absolute clarity about tricking him with her hospitality. Who would blame Jael if she had just waited for someone else to come along to do the job, or if she had hidden in what we might call a cloud of confusion. Instead she took decisive action. This is an example, though exceptional, of a woman using her God-given feminine and domestic role to glorify God. The Israelites destroyed Jabin king of Canaan.

The Inspiration of a Woman
It seems that Deborah was strictly a prophet and accompanied Barak to battle, but did not personally engage in combat. There would likely have been other women accompanying the army to act as cooks, nurses, and sundry helpers. There is no textual indicator that Deborah did anything other than support and endorse Barak's call to arms. Barak was primarily a military leader. Deborah was steady and wise in her dealings with people. Barak was given the vast undertaking of rallying troops and fighting an oppressor. I think Barak's challenge required a Deborah. He and his people were in a vicious historical cycle of disobedience—punishment—and repentance. Trusting God and believing his prophet would not come easily to a man whose generation "had not known the Lord or seen his works in Israel." Barak's job was unenviable!

Barak's victory was largely the result of Deborah's inspiration. Her prophetic encouragement kept him going when the enemy seemed insurmountable. She didn't want to leave her home or go to battle, though there is no mention of her fighting. As a woman leader, Deborah's unique mission was to bolster Barak. She wanted him to lead as a man. Sometimes women have to support godly men in this way. I suspect that Deborah went back home and gladly surrendered to her husband's leadership.

The Courage of a Woman
Today we need the courage and clarity of Deborah in our homes, neighborhoods, schools, churches, and workplaces. How commonplace it has become for women to morally falter when the right behavior and decisions used to be expected of women! It has historically been the high moral standards of women who determine the success of nations. As those standards fall, so goes the fabric of society.

The heart of wisdom is clarity—the insight of crystal clear truth and a commitment to do the right thing no matter what! This was

Deborah's greatest leadership skill. If we today want to be like her we must be prepared to be misunderstood. We must seek after God and surround ourselves with other like minded women. As in Deborah's day, morality is now seen as outmoded; heroism is scorned; truth is insufferable; and drawing a line in the sand is reviled. Love has come to mean nothing more than niceness.

The Song of Deborah and Barak
Throughout Scripture (see my study on Eve) it is clear that God's creative pattern is for men to be the primary leaders in the home and church. Because of sin this plan is challenging for both men and women. It is important for women with strong personalities to not over power or show up the men. Deborah is a good model of this. Her leadership might have been partly due to the lack of strong godly men at the time. Barak is God's chosen, but his confidence and daring isn't what it should be. Since he asked, or pleaded, for Deborah to remain with him, she must have had a motivational effect as the results clearly indicate. Today's women would love to tap into that! Reassurance is what our pastors and leaders need, not berating or undermining. No doubt, Deborah told the truth, but in a manner that could be well received. And she was God's prophetess. Her assertions were as compelling as her God!

When Deborah and Barak sing their song of praise to God, they poetically recount the victorious events of the battle. They celebrate the bravery of those who fought and curse those tribes who refused to come to the help of the Lord (5:23). The last few verses pay tribute to the cunning and bravery of Jael. It is she, a woman, who had the spirit and precision to slay the enemy. A woman doing her work at home in her tent, utilizing hospitality and household tools, to strike the enemy. God's ways sometimes seem inequitable to our fallible judgment, but he saw to it that in this song sung by Deborah and Barak that the honor for bravery went to the right person in Judges 5:4, "Most blessed of women is Jael, the wife of Heber the Kenite, of tent-dwelling women most blessed...She sent her hand to the tent peg...she struck Sisera; she crushed his head; she shattered and pierced his temple." And the land had rest for forty years.

Barak's Humility
Much credit should be given to Barak for his willingness to be receptive to a woman. Instead of wondering how to have more leadership roles, we women should be curious about Deborah's effectiveness with Barak. Was there something about her life which suggested to him that she was not competing with him? Was she known for her supportiveness toward her husband and other masculine leaders? Perhaps her willing subordination contributed to his eventual acceptance of God's will.

Where Are The "Deborahs"?
Deborah was a leader who gave people a vision of a God bigger than what had been seen in a long time. She was sought out for her ability to see clearly the truth and live by it. She was willing to confine her ministry as a prophetess to her own back yard and not above being a submissive wife. Deborah was not concerned about who got credit for Israel's victory. Ironically we don't know much about her own ministry under the palm, except as it pertains to her success at encouraging someone else in leadership. It is Barak who is credited with delivering the people of God in 1 Samuel 12:11. It is Barak and other judges who are noted for their faith in Hebrews 11:3.

When Deborah ventured from home it was to support the leadership of Barak whose job it was to deliver God's people. When the Israelites failed in their faithfulness to God, it began a crisis of leadership which lasted throughout the period of the judges. It was a crisis of manhood. Of men who gave up worship of the living, One True God, for an idol. Men who had been emasculated by their worship of a fertility statue!

Deborah's leadership is what I would call an indictment on those men, not an example of women doing everything men can do. In fact, her ministry was uniquely feminine and nurturing. Barak was faithfully trying to save his people from bondage, and did in the end. Deborah built him up with the truth of God's promises. In today's world we have a similar challenge. Our men (husbands and other leaders) are living in a society that no longer values manhood, just domesticated males. It's easy for women to bash their men for not being strong enough when it is women themselves who have often done the emasculating.

We need to be Deborahs who have the godly perspective of our own leadership abilities and God given roles. Christian women should not be above playing subordinate or nurturing roles, even when we are displeased with those we support. Our families and churches will be best served when we get a sacrificial vision for helping our men to be victorious over their own self doubts. That will be victory for us all.

The prophetess in each of us, whatever her style or arena, is needed urgently. We live in our own land of declining morality and rising paganism. Each day is filled with big and small opportunities to speak and model the truth of God's word to loved ones and acquaintances. Women everywhere, in and outside of the church, are in need of clarity from Scripture and Christian friendship. The gods of self are finding a stronghold among a new generation of women. How can we continue to hide from the threat? It is not enough for godly women to be good. We must enter the battle, as prayerful women who support the good and uphold the truth. That will be victory for us all!

Questions for Study and Discussion:

1. From the first three chapters of Judges, approximately how many generations have gone by since the people of Israel entered Canaan? Why does it seem to be difficult for future generations (our children and grandchildren) to maintain a strong passion for God and not compromise spiritually and morally?

2. In Judges 4:1-2 we are told that God sold his disobedient people into the hand of the wicked king Jabin. What part does punishment play in God's scheme of things both then and now?

3. If people sought Deborah out for her wisdom and advice, what character traits do you believe she possessed.

4. Do you see any significance to the fact that her husband's name is given in 4:4? Please explain.

5. What are the implications, if any, for today's woman with leadership abilities?

6. Read Judges 4:4-14.

    How would you characterize Deborah's words to Barak?

    What was the result each time she spoke to him?

7. Who was the woman to whom the Lord gave the honor of killing Sisera?

8. In Judges 4:17-22 the account is given of this woman's deception and bravery. Even though we don't live in a time of war, or have cause to lure people into our homes to kill them, what qualities and principles can we learn from this account?

9. Judges 4:23-24 implies two important principles about

victory for the Christian:

Verse 23 tells us that the battle belongs to _____.

Verse 24 suggests that the battle was won, not by an individual hero, but by _____.

10. In the song of Deborah and Barak (5:28-30) there is an apt description of the erroneous perceptions of Sisera's mother and her companions when faced with battle and defeat. How could this be applied today to those who arrogantly pit themselves against the Lord? Read this passage and list some of those misperceptions and false hopes.

11. What modern day idols are we Christians facing?

12. What are you doing personally or as a family to combat the spiritual complacency that leads to compromise and idolatry?

13. What importance does having a biblical vision of womanhood and manhood play in the development of a leader?

14. From the life of Deborah, how can a woman be strong and yet submissive?

※※※※※※※※※※※※※※※※※※※※※※※※※※※※※※※※※

THE SHUNAMMITE WOMAN—COMPELLED BY GOD

※※※※※※※※※※※※※※※※※※※※※※※※※※※※※※※※※

Scripture Reference:
2 Kings 4:8-37 • 2 Kings 8:1-6

The prophet Elisha was the successor of Elijah. His miracle filled ministry was set during the reigns of a series of evil Israelite kings who provoked the Lord to anger. Our study takes place during the reign of Jehoram, one of Ahab's sons, "who did evil in the eyes of the Lord, but not as his father and mother had done." During this dark time of Israel's history, God sent prophets to warn his people of their sin and its consequences of famine and oppression.

On Mount Carmel Elijah had confronted the priests of Baal who were followed by King Ahab and his pagan wife Jezebel. His ministry was passed on to his servant Elisha who also carried on in faithful service to God. One day Elisha went to Shunem and was urged by a wealthy woman to stay for a meal. Whenever he passed through Shunem, Elisha would turn in there to eat.

A Wealthy Woman

The "wealthy" woman, as cited in 4:8, seems to be blessed with resources at a time when many of her neighbors are in the midst of famine or can remember a time of famine. She is not in material need. She is a believer and alert to the fact that Elisha is God's representative. In verse 9 she said to her husband, "Behold now, I know that this is a holy man of God who is continually passing our way. Let us make a small room on the roof with walls and put there for him a bed, a table, a chair, and a lamp, so that whenever he comes to us, he can go in there." These are the words of a spiritually sensitive and submissive woman. She wants to help the man of God and yet is respectful of her husband's role as head of the home. She shares her idea with him by painting a picture of the prophet's chambers. We will see as our study progresses that she is more youthful and able-bodied, but she speaks to her husband inclusively and encouragingly, not as a bossy wife. This approach evidently enhances her wifely influence with her husband. Perhaps this idea would be seen by her husband as a way to ensure more privacy for he and his wife!

This generosity on their part also suggests that the small family wants to be as close to the prophet as possible. They want him to spend more time with them. They are open to a deeper relationship with him and his God

The Hidden Need
As a result, verse 11 tells us that the next time the prophet visited, a special chamber on the roof had been prepared and he rested in it. How does one repay or show gratitude to one so capable and generous? His hostess is not a needy woman looking for something in return. Elisha has to probe into her needs. He asks his servant Gehazi to speak to her (due to a language barrier) and find out what can be done for her. Her answer is not much help. She is fine as she is and doesn't need anything. Well, this certainly does seem to be the case on the surface. But when she leaves, Elisha asks Gehazi his opinion. In verse 14 he says, "Well she has no son, and her husband is old." Elisha, in all his prophetic wisdom and compassion instantly knows what to do for this nurturing and generous woman: he calls her back to his chamber to tell her that this time next year she will embrace a son.

Except for her childlessness, this woman is not in need. She can welcome others into her home and give generously. She is her own woman even though she is a submissive wife. She and her husband have the money and resources to build an addition onto their home. If a woman like this is going to have a need, it will be a giant, something no one can supply. She must have resigned herself long ago to barrenness. And then the holy man of God to whom she has been drawn prophecies something beyond anything she could hope for.

The woman's response of "No…do not lie to your servant," is to beg to be excused from disappointment. To believe the prophet and his word might be too much of a risk. Have you ever wanted something so badly, yet assumed it would never be possible? In spite of her fear, she conceived and bore a son about that time the following spring, as Elisha had told her. As with the Shunammite woman, we don't get to choose our blessings or select God's promises. Those things are under his control.

We might imagine the delight the Shunammite couple would have in raising their son. Their feelings of devotion and respect for Elisha would only grow as the prophet continued to visit them and become familiar with their son. Perhaps the boy would grow in affection towards the godly prophet. There must have been a loving relationship between Elisha and this family.

Helplessness
The following account is found in 4:18-31. When the child was older he went out one day to his father among the reapers. Evidently having a sun stroke, he cried, "Oh, my head, my head!" And the father said to his servant, "Carry him to his mother." The servant lifted the boy and brought him to his mother who held him in her lap until noon. He then died. This is horrifying to envisage for this woman. Her son promised by God and made possible by God is now dead. Maybe at first she thought he would get over a little sun stroke. Perhaps she thought he was sleeping, and then realized he was lifeless. How could this be the end for her miracle child!

Back to The Word
In verse 1 the bereaving mother does a bizarre thing. She takes the body of her son up to the prophet's chamber and lays him on the

bed, shuts the door, and leaves. I believe this woman wanted her son to be as close to God as possible. This act symbolizes going back to the Word of God and the origin of God's promises. Right then and there this woman has decided to count on God to make good on his promises to her.

She returns the child to the place where he was promised to her. We too should take our broken dreams and wounds to God's Word. We need to see problems and crises from His perspective. We need the Shunammite's gutsy determination to hold on to God's promises.

Tenacious Prayer

Then she calls to her husband and says, "Send me one of the servants and one of the donkeys, that I may quickly go to the man of God and come back again." Her husband evidently doesn't understand the urgency of the situation or the purpose of her wish to travel. He questions her for wanting to make a near twenty five mile journey at such a time. She doesn't waste time or energy. She doesn't weaken her resolve by making explanations. Her husband will eventually discover for himself the necessity of her demands. She assures her husband, "All is well." She has great faith, but it is not inert. She will not be satisfied until she reaches Elisha.

If we women could somehow replicate for ourselves the Shunammite's sense of urgency! Do we have to be holding the lifeless body of a child to sense the necessity of prayer and claiming God's promises? We must realize that our most important role as women is that of praying for our families. It is a release and a privilege for us to "pray at all times in the Spirit, with all prayer and supplication for all the saints...." (Eph. 6:18)

I believe the Shunammite woman's journey to find Elisha is symbolic of our journey of prayer. Notice that she knew where to find the prophet. She somehow knew that he could be found at Mt. Carmel. They had a relationship she could and would presume upon. It is also our benefit as God's children to be able to presume upon our intimacy with Him. Do you cultivate such a relationship with God? Don't wait until tragedy strikes. Foster a daily time of prayer and seeking after God so that you will have a well worn path to Him!

When Elisha saw the woman coming, he sent his servant Gehazi to meet her and ask after her family. Her answer: "All is well." When she reached the man of God she caught hold of his feet. When Gehazi starts to push her away the prophet corrects him and says in verse 27, "Leave her alone, for she is in bitter distress, and the Lord has hidden it from me and has not told me." Even Elisha is dependant upon God's revelation and power.

Once again, I believe the significance of her answer, "All is well," is that she has a vital sense of faith in God despite the circumstances. She is compelled to get as close as she can to God, through the prophet. Her behavior is unsettling and probably improper. But the prophet himself is compelled by her faith. This is a woman who has never before been desperate for anything, so now she must be taken seriously.

Intervention

In verse 8 the faithful yet frantic woman says to Elisha, "Did I ask my lord for a son? Did I not say, 'Do not deceive me?'" In other words, "This whole thing was God's idea, not mine!" Elisha instantly understands her plight and sends Gehazi ahead to minister healing with his prophet's staff. But this does not satisfy the woman. She tells Elisha, "As the Lord lives and as you yourself live, I will not leave you." At this point it may be that God has enabled his prophet to understand the woman's language in the absence of Gehazi. So he arose and followed her.

This woman won't settle for a little comfort or professional help. She knows she needs a miracle. She knows that miracles require God and His presence is in the holy man of God. When Gehazi returns to meet them he reports that the child has not awakened. I wonder if God was leading Elisha to just allow the situation to unfold as an object lesson for future generations. He must have known that the staff in itself had no power.

When Elisha comes into the house he sees the child lying dead on his bed. As told in verses 32 through 37, he first closes the door and begins praying to the Lord. Then he laid on the child, putting his mouth on his mouth, his eyes on his eyes, and his hands on his hands. As he stretched out on the child this way, the flesh of the child became warm. Then he walked back and forth in the house and went back up and stretched himself back onto the child again. The child sneezed seven times opened his eyes. Then Elisha summoned Gehazi and said, "Call this Shunammite."

Our Need
I believe this skin to skin contact between Elisha and the boy is symbolic of our need for spiritual resuscitation. It's not enough for one to rely on self improvement or leave it to chance. Notice that even the prophet's staff couldn't revive the dead child. The only thing that could awaken the child from death was the power of God through the prophet. The prophet here represents the redeeming blood of Jesus. We must be fully covered by the sacrificial blood of Jesus who died for our sins. The expertise of man will fail us. The best intentions of philosophy will fall short. There is no magical icon that can save us from sin and death. The only hope we have is the intervention of God on our behalf by sending Jesus to die on the cross for our sin.

This woman's faith was greatly rewarded when the prophet brought the boy to life, sent for her and said, "Pick up your son." She surely didn't understand all the future theological implications, but she knew she was experiencing the supernatural power of God. As verse 37 says, "She came and fell at Elisha's feet, bowing to the ground. Then she picked up her son and went out." Her trust in God and His promises was justified. Her vigilance in prayer was rewarded.

God's Greater Purpose
At what point this occurred, we are not certain, but sometime later Elisha told the woman to take her family and sojourn wherever

she could, for the Lord had called for a famine which would last seven years. This account is in 2 Kings 8:1-6. She "arose and did according to the word of the man of God. She went with her household and sojourned in the land of the Philistines seven years." This implies that her husband, son, and servants left property behind to eke out a humble living by moving around from place to place as needed. This was often done by God's people when struck by famine. The text suggests that their property was requisitioned and utilized by the government to feed the people of their famine stricken land.

The Shunammite woman "did according to the word of the man of God." She already knew that she could count on God. Not only does she act in faith by leaving behind productive property in the care of someone else, she demonstrates faith by returning from the land of the Philistines at the end of seven years according to the word of Elisha. She returns to the king to claim what is hers.

Restoration
Thus far we have seen this woman in a state of helpless desperation when she went to the prophet to raise her son. Then we viewed God's intervention when the child was raised. Now we are witness to the complete restoration of this woman and her family to what is rightfully theirs. We see in verse 4 that Elisha's servant Gehazi just happens to be chit chatting with the king when the woman comes in to make her appeal for her house and her land. After the king listens to the woman, Gehazi points out that this is the woman whose son Elisha raised. When the woman verifies this to the king, he appoints an official to, "restore all that was hers, together with all the produce of the fields from the day that she left the land until now." Because of the Shunammite's moving testimony the king felt compelled to reimburse her for all the revenue that the land produced for the crown during her absence.

I believe the application for us here is that our problems and even our very lives are not just about us. God is orchestrating events and history to bring about his plan. His ultimate plan is about bringing glory to Himself. He uses various tools to do this, including our pain, failures, successes, and sufferings. When the Shunammite woman first offered food to Elisha she would have had no idea that God's real aim was to establish a relationship between her and the prophet that would permit him the presumption of claiming her property. Everything that happened in between was simply leading to that point. And now that she has been compelled by God and had a compelling effect on others, she is privileged to experience complete restoration: Her family residence and finances reinstated. Yet, there is greater abundance in her life now than there was before she knew tragedy. She now knows God intimately and has a son.

There are any number of resources, talents, and abilities in our lives that God may have his eye on. As in the case of the Shunammite's son and property, He has the right to do with us as he deems fit for the good of His kingdom. On the way there are many lessons we need to learn that we can't anticipate. Every good deed or tragedy is an opportunity for us to trust His Word and pray for His will; a future day for those compelled by God to claim His promises and cling to His Word.

Questions for Study and Discussion:

1. See 2 Kings 4:8. This story begins with a generous woman giving to Elisha during a time of famine. She and her husband continue to offer hospitality to Elisha. How would you describe her just based on verses 8-17?

2. Do you see this woman as expecting reward or recognition for her deeds?

3. How would you characterize the mother's behavior when she decides to go to Elisha on behalf of her son? How does this symbolize the need for prayer?

4. Has there ever been a time in your life when you were determined to find spiritual help, but sensed or experienced someone presenting roadblocks as in the case of Gehazi in verse 7? Do you let this become an excuse for quitting?

5. In verse 28 through 30 the woman expresses her frustration to the prophet Elisha. Could you put her words into your own paraphrase?

6. When the woman takes her son up to the prophet's chamber, how can we do the same with crisis and urgent needs?

7. It wasn't an easy thing for Elisha to restore life to the boy, what does the difficulty and effort involved symbolize about salvation? (2 Kings 4:32-37)

8. In Kings 8:6 the Shunammite woman is assured by the king of something that God assures us in Psalm 23:3. Though we will have to suffer and see disappointment in life, what guarantee is there for the believer?

MARTHA AND MARY: LEARNING FROM JESUS

Scripture References:
Luke 10:1-12—Jesus sends out the 72 disciples
Luke 10:38-42—Martha has Jesus in her home
John 11—Death of Lazarus, Jesus Raises Lazarus, Sanhedrin Plots to kill Jesus
Matthew 26:1-16 anointing
Mark 14:1-11 anointing
John 12:1-8 anointing

In Luke 10 Jesus appointed seventy two disciples to go two by two into "every town and place where he himself was about to go." These disciples are in addition to the twelve closest disciples, perhaps their disciples. He gave explicit instructions to these disciples as to the urgency of their purpose and what their personal conduct should be towards those who would receive them in each town. They were even told in Luke 10:10 how to take rejection: "If you enter a town and they do not receive you, go into its streets and say, 'Even the dust of your town that clings to our feet we wipe off against you. Nevertheless know this that the kingdom of God has come near.' I tell you, it will be more bearable on that day for Sodom than for that town."

When the seventy two return with joy because of their success, Jesus gently directs them to be happy for a different reason. He tells them in verse 20 to rejoice in the privilege of serving God. The results are in His hands. The joy is in pleasing and obeying him "that your names are written in heaven." Then, in that same hour Jesus rejoices in prayer and exclaims in 10: that "no one knows who the Son is except the Father, or who the Father is except the Son and anyone to whom the Son chooses to reveal him." This prepares the way for Jesus' visit to the village of Bethany.

The Long Awaited Visitor
God has chosen to reveal himself to a family in the village of Bethany when Jesus visits there. Perhaps this village had already been visited by Jesus' advance men. This is our introduction to the family of Lazarus; it is their introduction to Jesus. Their home would be the hub of activity during Jesus' stay in Bethany. Martha would have spent days, perhaps weeks planning and preparing to give a great show of hospitality to Jesus and his fellow travelers.

To open your home to the one reputed to be the Messiah would be a task of great anticipation. "What is his message about the kingdom of God?" she and Mary would wonder. To have a great teacher in their home would indeed be a privilege for the sisters. In the traditional synagogues and communities in which Jesus concentrated his ministry, women were not directly taught by rabbis. Synagogues were the place of learning for men and their sons. But the home was the domain of women. The women present would be able to see and hear Jesus speak first hand. In one's own home a woman could interact with a guest more directly.

Luke 10:38-39 states that Martha welcomed Jesus into her home. Her sister named Mary sat at the Lord's feet and listened to his teaching. To "sit at the feet" of a teacher is a figure of speech which means that Mary was receiving the words of Jesus. We don't know if she was the only student, or if she was one of many. The text implies that Mary was absorbing like a sponge the teaching of Jesus. Luke 10:40 says, "Martha was distracted from much serving". This suggests that Martha could have set everything aside for Jesus along with Mary and the others.

The Teacher
This visit with Jesus in her home was probably Martha's first encounter with Jesus. If so, how is she yet to know that he is

more than just an esteemed teacher? Even if she knew that he was bringing in the kingdom of God, how would that translate to everyday life? For some reason Martha is not part of the group sitting at Jesus' feet. Or perhaps she was jealous of Mary sitting with him alone. At this point her serving has become a distraction for her. In her distraction, or serving, she becomes isolated. In her isolation she becomes resentful. She directs her resentment toward her sister who isn't helping her. When she takes her concerns to Jesus, his answer to Martha is a gentle rebuke in verse 41, "Martha, Martha, you are anxious and troubled about many things, but one thing is necessary. Mary has chosen the good portion, which will not be taken away from her."

Much has been said about Jesus' reply to Martha. I will focus on what the text says and not on a conventional message about "serving verses listening."

Jesus' words solicit these questions: What was it that Mary was choosing? What was so great about sitting at Jesus' feet? And what is it that won't be taken from her? It is very simple: Mary was receiving from Jesus. She was compelled by something about him to listen and focus on him. Like all of us when God decides to get our attention—we listen, or "sit at his feet" and let him unfold to us who He is. But Martha was not yet a party to this. She was just serving an honored guest. She was trying to give something of value. She was making a noble effort to do something completely impossible: impress God. Martha's serving was distracting her from knowing Jesus. In other words, "Martha, of all you have been busy doing, you have failed to do the most important thing! Mary has chosen the one necessary thing, and it will not be taken away from her."

Jesus' visit to Bethany is about much more than serving verses listening. It is about knowing God verses not knowing Him. Martha didn't know it at first, but when she approached Jesus with her complaint he was actually drawing her to himself—as he had already been doing with Mary. He exposed her faulty, unredeemed attitude. He was filling her in on the teaching she had been missing out on while she fumed over pots and pans.

Here is my own paraphrase to show how I think this should be applied to us today:

> "Martha, Martha, you are very busy, skilled, and frustrated. Even though you spend your time doing good things, don't you know that I am here? There is nothing you can say or do that matters as much as the fact that I am simply here with you. I have come to save you. I have come to give you Myself. I am the long awaited Messiah. Let me show you my glory. Come and taste the food of my Father. It is not about what you can give, but what you can receive from me. I am the one necessary thing! You belong with me just like Mary. I want to include you in my kingdom!"

Mary chose to hear Jesus reveal himself to her. Mary let other things go to grab hold of eternal life in Jesus. When Martha compared herself to her sister basking in the glow of Jesus, she envied her. She became aware of her own emptiness. I believe Martha would also humble herself to learn from Jesus. She too would come to know and be close to him. She would find that she and her sister could belong to Jesus equally. There would be new meaning to her life and service to others. Having been met with Jesus intimately, she can now truly serve him. And it would not be taken away from her either. Jesus was not like other leaders of his day. He taught women freely, even when they didn't expect it.

Salvation

Whatever our talents, skills, achievements, or failures—we all have one great need. That great need is the void in our lives that can only be filled by Jesus. Only Jesus can save us from our bad attitudes, destructive behavior, or wrong doing known as sin. Sometimes when things are going well, the void is easily overlooked. But even if things are going well and your goals are being met, without a one-on-one relationship with Jesus deep down inside, you won't shake that nagging sense of emptiness. Until one is met by the loving words of Jesus: Martha, Martha let Me be the most important thing in your life! The beauty of Jesus' visit to Bethany is that He engaged each woman in a manner according to her individual personality. He still does that today. I believe Martha shifted from "serving portions" to receiving Jesus as her never ending portion.

Jesus, the Guest Who Offends
When Jesus came to visit the family of Lazarus, it would be fitting for the hostess to expect that her role is to give to Him. Martha would naturally believe she is to be the one imparting gracious hospitality to Jesus. But Jesus' surprised her with a paradigm shift. When the Messiah comes, he is the giver! We realize our own poverty when faced with his overflowing riches. We see our own formerly impressive efforts in a new light when faced with the brilliance and purity of Jesus. I believe we are all like Martha, not by personality, but by our soul poverty which is so well disguised. Mary is the model of a woman recognizing immediately that Jesus is the One with everything to give. We need humility to receive from this Guest the brilliance and purity He has to offer. I believe we are all like Martha, not by personality, but by our soul poverty, which is so well disguised. Mary is the model of a woman recognizing immediately that Jesus is the One with everything to give. We need humility to receive from this Guest!

"I and the Father Are One"
Now we will turn to John 10:22 to see the mounting opposition Jesus faces in his ministry. When the Jerusalem Jews at the temple during the Feast of Dedication (also known as Hanukkah) gathered around Jesus to press Him on whether or not He was the Christ, Jesus rebuked their unbelief. He tells them in John 10:7 that His sheep hear His voice, He knows them, and gives them eternal life, and they cannot be snatched from His hand. This implies that the cynicism of these sophisticates is not as

important to Jesus as the fact that God evidently has not chosen to reveal Himself to them. Jesus ends the dialogue in verse 30 with the fighting words, "I and the Father are one." The Jews pick up stones to stone him. When Jesus challenges their reasoning for wanting to stone him when all he has done is good works, they declare that they will stone him for blasphemy for claiming to be equal to God. This angry mob eventually tries to arrest Jesus, but He escapes from their hands.

In verse 40 Jesus goes to the place where John had baptized where he is received in faith. Across the Jordan, away from the politics of Jerusalem, "many believed in Him there."

The Death of Lazarus
In the midst of violent hostility on one hand and many coming to faith and salvation on the other hand, Jesus receives word from the sisters in Bethany. John 11 reveals the information in this sequence:

- Lazarus of Bethany was ill

- From the village of Mary and her sister Martha

- It was Mary who anointed the Lord with ointment and wiped his feet with her hair whose brother Lazarus was ill

- The sisters sent to him saying, "Lord, he whom you love is ill."

Jesus receives word from Bethany, which is approximately two miles from Jerusalem. What would have gone through his disciple's minds when they heard the message from the sisters of Lazarus saying, "Lord, he whom you love is ill"? I think they must have been saddened for their friends in Bethany, yet apprehensive that Jesus would want to go there. It wouldn't be safe for them to venture near Jerusalem. So, what an ambivalent relief for those men to hear Jesus' response to the message, "This illness does not lead to death. It is for the glory of God, so that the Son of God may be glorified through it." Likely, the disciples thought they were not going to have to tread dangerous territory. Maybe they talked amongst themselves about how great it was that Jesus was finally thinking strategically. They would never have guessed just how strategically Jesus was planning.

> John 11:5-7 says, "Now Jesus loved Martha, and her sister and Lazarus. So, when he heard that Lazarus was ill, he stayed two days longer in the place where he was. Then after this he said to the disciples, "Let us go to Judea again."

There is a crucial thing in these verses to observe: In verse 5 Jesus' love for the family of Lazarus is cited as His reason for staying two days longer. In other words, Jesus loved his friend so much that he let him die instead of hurrying back to save him. Does that sound like what you learned in Sunday school? "Jesus loves you, so He will sometimes not answer your prayers. He will allow you to suffer and die even though he could heal you, but it's because he loves you."

No, this is not taught in Sunday schools across the country, but it should be! One might wonder how this could coincide with the wonderful plan God has for everyone's life. Well, God had and still has a more far reaching goal in the universe than to just bless us or heal us. His chief aim is to bring glory to himself. His wonderful plan for you and me is to be glorified in our living and dying. Unbeknownst to his very dearest friends and disciples, Jesus knew that God would be more glorified if Lazarus died than if Lazarus was healed. Jesus is bringing about the circumstances that will set the stage for God to be mightily glorified.

Now, verses 8 through 15 imply that the disciples are still in denial about Lazarus' true condition. They have wanted to believe that what Jesus meant in verse 4 was that the sick man would get better. I doubt they just didn't care. When Jesus announces in verse 7, "Let us go to Judea again" the disciples are alarmed and try to talk him out of it by reminding him of the past efforts of the Jews to stone him. Anyone can see it would be too risky. Jesus assures them in verse 8 that they need not fear and hide from their enemies because they are in the light. It is his enemies who walk in the night who will stumble.

In John 11:11 Jesus puts things in perspective: "Our friend Lazarus has fallen asleep, but I go to awaken him." The disciples are slow to understand Jesus' metaphors, so he spells it out plainly: "Lazarus has died, and for your sake I am glad that I was not there, so that you may believe. But let us go to him." Thomas (in verse 16) in his cynical bravery says to his fellow disciples, "Let us also go, that we may die with him."

I Am the Resurrection and the Life
When Jesus reached Bethany Lazarus had been in the tomb four days. Since Bethany was only about two miles from Jerusalem many of the Jews from Jerusalem had come to Martha and Mary to grieve with them. John 11:20 indicates that Martha went to meet Jesus on the outskirts of the village as soon as she heard he was coming. She probably did not tell Mary, who remained seated in the house surrounded by consoling friends. Martha was the one informed of Jesus' coming, and she was either instructed to meet him or was sensitive to the need for discretion. The warrant for Jesus' arrest would not be a secret. Maybe she would have assumed this to be the reason for his late arrival. Clearly, Jesus' disciples want to keep a low profile. Jesus may have allowed this at first so that he could have private conversations with Martha and Mary.

Martha, always honest and bold, says to Jesus, "Lord, if you had been here, my brother would not have died. But even now I know that whatever you ask from God, God will give you." Then Jesus replies in John 11:25 "I am the resurrection and the life. Whoever believes in me, though he die, yet shall he live, and everyone who lives and believes in me shall never die. Do you believe this?" Her reply in verse 7, "Yes Lord; I believe that you are the Christ, the Son of God, who is coming into the world." Then Martha goes and calls for Mary, telling her privately that, "the Teacher is here and is calling for you."

The Teacher of Women
The words of Martha to Jesus tell us that she was a godly woman of faith. She is correct and insightful when she tells Jesus that she knows he could have saved her brother. And she is willing to be taught even further, in the midst of grieving, by the Lord himself. Jesus presses her for more than just agreement when he says, "Do you believe this?" He's asking for a confession of personal faith and he gets a vivid one. Jesus is stressing to Martha and us that He is the resurrection. She is not only to trust in the future resurrection of souls and Jesus' power to save, she is about to see resurrection take place!

Martha's words to Mary, "The Teacher is here and is calling for you" strongly imply that Martha and Mary share a love for Jesus because he is their teacher! They surely understand and accept their role as women. They will never be religious leaders or have a role as Jesus' apostles. But they can say that He is their teacher. Jesus took the time to relate to them and care about their concerns. He gives them each one on one attention and instruction, and He is moved by their grief. Until Jesus came along, most women in their village would never sit under the teaching of any male leader unrelated to them, or even have a conversation with one. But Jesus has proven to be different. They don't understand what He is doing in this instance concerning their brother, but they know they can trust him.

Moved in His Spirit
When Mary runs out to meet Jesus in the place where Martha left him (he and the disciples are still keeping a low profile!) she is followed by the Jews who were with her in the house, "supposing she was going to the tomb to weep there." Mary's words to Jesus in John 11:32 are filled with emotion, "Lord, if you had been here, my brother would not have died." When Jesus saw Mary and the

others weeping he was "moved in his spirit and greatly troubled." Jesus experienced heart felt grief for the loss of Lazarus. He really felt the suffering of Mary and Martha. Death is a tragedy. It is the result of sin. But I think Jesus also knew that he was about to do something which would be the thrust for his opponents to plan his death. He was grieving for Lazarus and anticipating his own imminent suffering.

When Jesus asks in 11:34, "Where have they laid him?" this must have been when the twelve disciples got really nervous. Now Jesus is taken by the gathering of mourners to the actual grave site. He weeps. Jesus is sensitive to the pain around him. I see three specific dynamics that touch Jesus at the scene of Lazarus' grave: First, he is stirred by the faith of Martha and Mary. All eyes are on him now as he goes to the tomb and openly weeps. Secondly, He must have been aware of those who were moved by and sharing in his grief referred to in 11:36. He knows that Lazarus' death has touched many people. Thirdly, there is cynicism from those who couldn't reconcile His love for Lazarus and his refusal to save him before he died. This kind of misperception would have been reason enough for Jesus to weep! Even for the Son of God, being misunderstood is painful.

The Glory of God

In John 11:38-44 Jesus comes to the tomb; a cave with a stone laid against it. He says, "Take away the stone." Martha, ever practical, says, "Lord, by this time there will be an odor, for he has been dead four days." Perhaps a reminder to Jesus that Lazarus is dead, really dead! Jesus says to her, "Did I not tell you that if you believed you would see the glory of God?" In essence: "I'm no longer mourning, I'm here to amaze!" I think Martha recalled Jesus' earlier words about resurrection. So they acted in faith and followed his orders.

Jesus lifted up his eyes and said, "Father, I thank you that you have heard me. I knew that you always hear me, but I said this on account of the people standing around, that they may believe that you sent me." When he had said these things, he cried out with a loud voice, "Lazarus, come out." The man who had died came out, his hands and feet bound with linen strips, and his face wrapped with a cloth. Jesus said to them, "Unbind him, and let him go."

Jesus knew that raising Lazarus from the dead would bring more glory and notice to God than merely healing him. But this meant Lazarus would have to endure illness and death. His sisters and loved ones would have to nurse him, watch him suffer, and see him dead and buried. These things would be staggering for the emotions of everyone involved, but from God's vantage point, nothing compared to the glory of raising a man from the grave. And this was far too much for some Jerusalem Jews to accept.

In John 11:45-53 we are told that many of the Jews from Jerusalem who had followed Mary to meet with Jesus and go to the tomb had seen what Jesus did and believed in him. But some of them "went to the Pharisees and told them what Jesus had done." This "snitching" led to the formalized death/arrest warrant for Jesus issued by the Sanhedrin, the supreme court of the Jewish people. They felt threatened by Jesus and for good reason. The more the crowds followed Him, the less power the Jewish officials had over the people. John 11:54 states that as a result of the edict against Him, Jesus no longer walked openly among the Jews. Jesus' mission would be fulfilled at a very specific, prophetic time.

His Death Foretold

From our standpoint, it is interesting to note that Matthew records two chapter's worth of Jesus prophesying to his disciples about the destruction of Jerusalem, the end times, and the final judgment. Then in Matthew 26:1-2 Jesus says to his disciples, "You know that after two days the Passover is coming, and the Son of Man will be delivered up to be crucified." This follows the account of a woman anointing Jesus with oil.

In Mark 13 we see the same kind of prophesying from Jesus to his disciples concerning their own persecution, the second coming of the Christ, and the final judgment. This also follows Mark's account of a woman anointing Jesus with oil. John does not record Jesus' prophecies concerning end times in the same way or sequence that Mark and Matthew do, but he does give the event of Lazarus dying and being raised as taking place in the same time frame as those prophecies.

John also tells us of a woman, named here as Mary of Bethany, who anoints Jesus with oil. Luke's only mention of Mary and Martha is in Luke 10. He does record in 7:36 the "sinful woman" who anoints Jesus, but this account is not to be confused with the other three. On this there is widespread agreement.

Three Versions, One Event

I believe that the accounts Matthew 6, Mark 14, and John 12, though Mary is only named in John, are the same account. There are scholars who have raised three obstacles to this. Not only do I think it remarkably improbable that Jesus and His disciples would have had this experience three separate times in one week, the so called obstacles are not difficult to surmount.

The three main difficulties of comparing these passages are as follows: 1) Location—John records the anointing at a dinner in Bethany with Martha serving. Matthew puts the dinner in the home of Simon in Bethany. Mark also puts the dinner at Simon's in Bethany. This is easy to overcome if you don't have a hard time believing that a dinner honoring Jesus might draw in the help and interest of several families who host and do the work together. I don't see a discrepancy.) Identity of women—Mary is only named in John, while Matthew and Mark record the anointing being done by "a woman." First, John also records the raising of Lazarus and would perhaps have been more familiar with Mary personally. It is possible that Matthew and Mark just didn't know the name of the woman who anointed Jesus, though the impression made by her was indelible. More importantly, the Matthew and Mark accounts focus on the obtuse reaction of the disciples, especially Judas' consequent decision to betray Jesus. John focuses on Mary's correct understanding of Jesus' imminent sacrifice. I see these differences as complimentary rather than contradictory. 3) Time—John 12:1 puts the dinner described as taking place probably on Friday evening, in Bethany (two miles from Jerusalem) two days before the holy week.

Matthew 26:2 gives the similar time frame of, "after two days the Passover is coming," which is not necessarily giving the time of the dinner which comes later, but spoken by Jesus when he finishes prophesying to the disciples, which I think refers to the week of Passover. Mark 14:1 states "it was two days before the Passover and the Feast of Unleavened Bread." He goes on to refer to the chief priests who have determined to wait until after the feast, or week of Passover, to arrest Jesus (the importance of this reference will be echoed later with Judas' betrayal). This gives the Matthew and Mark dinners as taking place on the same approximate day as the John account which would have been the Sabbath dinner, or Shabbat!

Though I believe the times given are different accounts referring to the same dinner, there are great and respected scholars who believe Matthew 26 to be a second account of an unknown woman. In consideration of that view, the following interpretation is flexible. The principles and applications are the same regardless.

The Disciples in Denial

As mentioned in John 11:55 the Jews are abuzz with curiosity about Jesus' whereabouts (now that he is in hiding in Ephraim, 11:54) and his intentions. Is he planning to come to Jerusalem for the week of Passover? Now that he has demonstrated His power, and infuriated the authorities by raising Lazarus, will He finally stick it to "the man," Jerusalem's corrupt establishment? It is now common knowledge, since the arrest warrant that Jesus is not on the road to rabbinical success, but onto something much grander.

So back to Bethany itself, the little haven in which Jesus' followers Lazarus, Martha, and Mary live. There is a Sabbath dinner given for him and his disciples in the home of Simon the Leper. There is a powerful sense of expectancy amongst the twelve in anticipation of going to Jerusalem. John tells us that "Martha served, and Lazarus was one of those reclining at table. Mary therefore took a pound of expensive ointment (eleven and a half ounces of pure nard) and anointed the feet of Jesus and wiped his feet with her hair." It is as if John wants us to know that everyone in this family is restored to their respective places in the family, fulfilling their role, previously made possible by the healing touch of Jesus. The alabaster flask in which the expensive oil would have been imported is broken to pour out all of the oil. None of it will be spared. This is emphasized by Matthew and Mark. It is clear from all the accounts that the disciples were not supportive of the act. An act of sacrifice which Jesus freely receives and defends!

Apostles in Training
Let's think about the mindset of the disciples. They have been through many highs and lows with Jesus. These young men have seen great miracles performed by Jesus as well as performing some on his behalf. They have given up earthly possessions and vocational prospects. They are intensely loyal to Jesus. They have seen his compassion. They've known his power and wisdom. They have enjoyed the prestige of being his Apostles. Prophecies of his death which seem clear to us now seem scarcely acknowledged by the disciples. They are used to being baffled by his strange words. They believe in him and love him deeply. They are ready to follow him into whatever battle and victory he has planned. A kingly triumph is what they anticipate for their visit to Jerusalem. They are naïve, but sincere.

But there is one among them who is not so devoted. There is one disciple whose love is tainted by greed and dishonesty. Matthew and Mark tell us that "the disciples" were indignant when Jesus was anointed by Mary. Mark tells us they went so far as to scold the woman. John tells us the leading critic was Judas, "because he was a thief and used to help himself to the money bag." Perhaps Judas was actually put in charge of the money bag! The other disciples needed to be set straight by Jesus.

Mary's Godward Thinking

Conversely, there is Mary who has been listening to and hanging onto every word spoken by or quoted of Jesus. She has perhaps discussed these things with Martha as the two of them have both been privileged to know Jesus and sit at his feet. We know that prior to this event Jesus' teaching concerning his own death was explicit. Were Jesus' own apostles in training possibly less objective and reflective than Mary? With the exception of Judas and his influence, I don't see their lack of understanding as anything other than denial of painful reality. How could they have understood more than they did? How could they have embraced Jesus' death? As leaders they were concerned about their own roles, their own ministry plans. They didn't want their master to diminish in power! His rise and demise would be theirs as well!

There is something especially advantageous to the feminine response to Jesus. When a woman is not too proud to serve others, supportive of the manly leadership around her, and in tune to the voice of God in her life—she has a heightened capacity for loving God. As a woman Mary didn't need to think about how Jesus' death would alter her career plans. She wasn't prone to jockey for the best position should the plans succeed wildly. She was free to just listen to Him and worship Him for Himself.

Mary's greatest aspirations were symbolized in the alabaster flask which held the precious oil. I can only imagine that as Mary listened to Jesus on various occasions and heard stories of his ministering she started to put it all together. With the growing hostility toward Jesus from the authorities, it would only be a matter of time before something would have to give. Either Jesus would have to put down his enemies or be put down by them. The twelve are expectant of the former, but Jesus has made it clear that He will die and their lives will be changed forever.

The ability for Mary to more fully absorb the meaning of Jesus' teaching would be the result of Godward thinking: "Lord, if Jesus is speaking literally, why would you allow the Romans to crucify him? For the same reason you allowed Lazarus to die? To show us your power? Would you really demonstrate your power in the death of Jesus? At this time, the time of Passover... the Passover Lamb! Will your resurrection power be with him in the end as it was at Lazarus' tomb?"

Practically, Mary must have wondered who would possibly dare to deliver Jesus to the chief priests. Certainly their loyal huddle of followers would be a safe haven for them all. Perhaps these folks would share in or eventually understand her dawning realizations. What would all of this signify for Jesus' disciples? Arrest, death, failure? Looking at Lazarus she knew their mission was in the control of a God who does the unexpected. She'd seen God's power when Jesus raised her brother. Martha told her that Jesus said, "I AM THE RESURRECTION...."

In the security of the gathering, and the tumult of her thoughts and prayers, Mary must have seen the truth with clarity. In the light of the eternal kingdom of God her dreams of marriage, home, and family seemed miniscule. Dead or resurrected, how could life without Jesus here be normal or ordinary ever again anyway? Their family may have discussed these implications at home. Mary would have confided in Martha about the precious oil she brought from home.

Mary's Devotion Unbound

As Mary looked down at the alabaster flask she held in her trembling hands, she would have thought of all the dreams it symbolized— All the longings of her feminine heart to have a godly husband who might be a leader in the synagogue—children and a home of her own to manage. Yes, even more than the precious oil, given to her by her family as a dowry, Jesus meant everything to her. Even if it meant sacrificing her dreams, she would follow him no matter what. She would believe in his sacrifice and resurrection with no reservations! Surely his death, even his death, would lead to God's glory. That would be her dearest dream—to live for his glory. While Jesus is surrounded by his disciples and her family, she will demonstrate her love and faith for his imminent sacrifice.

While breathing a prayer, Mary tenderly approaches Jesus while he reclines at the table. The room becomes silent as she kneels down at his side. Everyone senses the urgency she feels. As Mary smashes the neck of the alabaster flask on the stone floor, she looks Jesus directly in the face. She sees love and compassion in his eyes. He puts her at ease by closing his eyes and remaining still. Mary begins to pour the expensive ointment on the Savior starting with his head, working her way down to his feet. She pours out her dowry, her chance for marriage, her future as a bride. When the flask is emptied of its aromatic contents she then unbinds her long hair which may never be unbound for a groom and uses it as a towel to wipe Jesus' feet. His beautiful tanned, calloused feet with which he has traveled many miles to preach, teach, and heal. He is the Lord. He is the Lord.

She hears a growing murmur in the room. Perhaps the others don't understand. Of course they wouldn't! She knows this is strange behavior from a modest Jewish maiden—hair streaming loose, strong with the aroma of the pure nard, and tears flowing unrestrained. Conscious of the terrible sight she must seem, Mary sits anxiously at Jesus' feet holding the broken empty jar. "I've done it for you, Lord," she is thinking. And Jesus looks at her lovingly as if he hears her very thoughts.

But there are other thoughts circulating in the room too. Some of the disciples are grumbling about the cost of Mary's perfume—that she was wasting it. Others are just critical of her lavish display. But Jesus, aware of this speaks up for all to hear, "Why do you trouble the woman! For she has done a beautiful thing to me. For you always have the poor with you, but you will not always have me. In pouring this ointment on my body, she has done it to prepare me for my burial. Truly, I say to you, wherever this gospel is proclaimed in the whole world, what she has done will also be told in memory of her." (Matthew 26:10-13)

How was the rebuke received by the men? I think they must have been stunned. But Mary was defended by her Lord. That would have been all the strength a woman needs. The room was filled with the beautiful fragrance of Mary's greatest hope and dream, Jesus and his joy—His joy at being understood, something rare for him. His disciples understood later. They remembered his words and told these accounts of Mary's visionary faith, even at their own expense.

Prophecy Fulfilled
This was a turning point for Judas. Now that he sees the money bag dwindling he searches for a new source of income. Matthew and Mark tell us that Judas goes to the chief priests (Sanhedrin) who had earlier determined in Mark 14:2 to put off Jesus' apprehension until after the Passover week. They knew that Jesus would be difficult to find and impossible to arrest in a crowd. Now, they have a covert ally in one of his own disciples. Judas receives thirty pieces of silver, more than he will be able to pilfer anytime soon from the collective money bag. Ironically, the one who betrays Jesus, also unwittingly makes it possible for the Son of God to be sacrificed as the Passover Lamb—The Lamb who was prepared for burial by a woman of courage, clarity, and compassion.

Mary's Abandon
Not only are we challenged by Mary's insight and vision of Christ and His mission. We are given an example of lavish love demonstrated with abandon. Not only was Mary willing to sacrifice something for Jesus. She was sacrificing her best possession. Not only did that possession become a sacrifice for her, but for her whole family and the disciples. She could have donated the flask of oil to Jesus' ministry. Mary could have sacrificed secretly or with less flamboyance. I sense in Mary a compelling flair for communicating truth without much consideration for public approval. As a woman she couldn't preach the truth, but she could live it. She couldn't possibly verbalize her intuitive grasp of Jesus' mission, but she could display it visually. She couldn't compensate Jesus for his love and sacrifice, but she could offer her own gratitude. Mary did something we should all do in response

Martha and Mary—Learning from Jesus

to her Lord: she loved Him with complete abandon.

Femininity Unbound

The message of Martha and Mary's lives is more than what I expected. Serve God unreservedly in whatever way you can and he will decide how to use it. Martha did this by practicing hospitality and humble service. She wasn't perfect in all she did, just willing to give and grow. Initially, our efforts may be clumsy or misguided, but God will correct and teach us through his word and other mature believers. It is better to learn as you go than to waste away theorizing on how you would like to use your gifts. Be a Martha and just serve with a heart that's teachable. There are so many opportunities that require humble service, which is sadly a dying art. Martha was a servant who became humble thanks to Jesus.

There is also a still deeper truth to learn from Martha and Mary's first visit from Jesus. Our initial response to Jesus must be to receive, not give. Human pride desires to clean up and appear worthy for the visit. But God comes into our lives to show us our need for him. As Hebrews 4:13 says, "...but all are naked and exposed to the eyes of him to whom we must give account." There is no fooling God or covering up. Jesus knocks on the door of our hearts so that we can be saved, forgiven, blessed, and dazzled by his greatness. Not so that we can impress him. To try and impress the Lord is a frustrating and futile effort. At some point we must all see the Martha in ourselves and receive from Jesus. Only then can our service be truly humble and glorifying to God.

I don't think we can understand Mary separately from Martha. Yes, we should all imitate Mary's penchant for sitting at Jesus' feet and listening to His word. But is that at the expense of doing the serving that Martha did? Are we women divided into Martha personalities and Mary types? Do we settle for the conventional thought that says we should try to find a balance between the two? I can't settle for that! If we listen carefully to these passages we have studied, there is a fuller meaning. When one looks at our society and sees the raging assault on traditional roles for women, the message of Martha and Mary begs to be heeded. I don't think they have two things, or separate things to say. From the time they met Jesus their voices, along with those of other holy women, have cried out in one unified call across the ages to us.

Freedom to Serve
The plea is for women to throw themselves into serving and loving Jesus with all our hearts and minds—and to do so passionately, together, in harmony, as redeemed women. Not as neutered leaders trying to minimize their God-given femininity, but as New Testament women, like Martha and Mary who find their identity in Christ and their greatest asset their uniquely feminine call to be nurturers. A femininity that leads the way in humble service to family and community. A femininity that finds its beauty in sacrifice for others. A femininity that does not recoil from transparency. A femininity that expresses itself in beautifully lavish submission to Christ!

The Bethany sisters probably never had positions of leadership in the emerging church. They learned from Jesus and presumably his Apostles. They cooked for them, served them, did women's work together, and fulfilled their nurturing roles while the men led. Some might think it a shame that these women from ancient times weren't granted more equality in roles. It would never have occurred to them to switch roles with the men. It doesn't seem to have occurred to Jesus either.

And yet, the freeing effect of their submission is an indictment on post modern pretensions of emancipation. When Mary was listening at Jesus' feet, she was compelling her lost sister to the same voice. When Martha was serving at the Sabbath dinner she was also serving on behalf of Mary who would anoint Jesus for burial. A burial that they anticipated. It's not that they were smarter or better than the men. They were just freed from the burden and concerns of leadership. Mary was at liberty as a woman to ingest all that Jesus said and did for its own sake. No spin, no career goals; just a daughter of God engrossed in His every word out of love for Him. A love that was shared by the sisters. Their sisterhood was sweet!

Martha and Mary call us to a uniquely feminine devotion to Christ Jesus for which today's generation of women long. If we in the church abandon the call, then who will be left to sit at the feet of her Savior with no sermon to prepare, just to revel in His glory? Who will be eager to host gatherings for folks to study the Bible? Who will be willing to partake in the womanly art of visiting the tomb of Jesus on Easter morning while the leaders strategize? Who will be brave enough to tell of the Resurrection? Who will be the "Titus Woman" with time to teach younger women to love their husbands and children? Who will be the true daughters of Sarah who make themselves beautiful with submission in a world of brash self seekers? Who will just be a woman!

Questions for Study and Discussion:

1. The family of Martha, Mary, and Lazarus seem to have been prominent and active in their Jewish community. What are ways in which women can make their homes, talents, and other resources available for ministry?

2. How does "knowing Jesus" impact one's serving? Learning from Martha's experience in Luke 10:38, what advantages do Christian women have in the following verses to steer us clear of resentment?

   1 Samuel 16:7

   Matthew 6:19-21

   Proverbs 17:22

   Psalm 66:18

   Galatians 6:8-10

3. How would you paraphrase the words of Jesus to Martha in Luke 10:42-43?

4. What is "the portion that will not be taken away" from those who know Jesus?

5. The King James Version of John 11:6 uses the phrase "Jesus tarried two days longer" to describe the Lord taking his time to respond to Lazarus.

   What is required of us when God decides to "tarry" when we have a serious need?

   What does John 11:35 suggest about Jesus and his emotional connection with those who follow him?

6. In John 11:5 Jesus says "I am the resurrection and the life…"

What do those words mean for us today?

What was Martha's response?

7. The author of this study uses the phrase "Godward thinking" to describe what Mary's thought process might have been. In light of 1 Thessalonians 5:17 what is Godward thinking?

8. Assuming that the three accounts in Matthew 26, Mark 14, and John 1 are of Mary anointing Jesus, what character traits could you list to describe Mary?

9. What would Mary's anointing ministry to Jesus have meant to Him? Do leaders need something from those to whom they minister? Explain your perspective.

10. As a godly young woman, Mary was willing to take the risk of vulnerability when she anointed Jesus. Discuss or list ways in which women today are also vulnerable when we give our hopes and dreams to God?

8

THE PROVERBS 31 WOMAN: AN EXCELLENT WIFE

Scripture Reference:
Proverbs 31
Hebrews 13:1-2
1Peter 4:7-11

Long ago in Israel, a young king received an urgent letter from his mother. He cringed with remorse as the servant handed him the letter with his mother's royal seal. He knew his mother wasn't happy with him of late. He was not living in the conscientious manner in which he had been raised. Rumors must have reached his loving but firm mother concerning his questionable friends and lifestyle.

The letter read:

Dear Son,

Your escapades with women and strong drink have come to my notice. My son, what are you doing? What are you doing, my son? Your father placed his hope and confidence in you!
Don't waste your life on those women who use you and don't love you. It will destroy your ability to find and love a good woman.
It is not for kings, O Lemuel, to get drunk and hide from responsibility. By doing this you destroy all the work that has been done by your father and cause great suffering for the poor.

If anyone should have strong drink it is those near death and those who have no hope. Stop feeling sorry for yourself and save your pity for those who have to depend on you! Use your position and privilege for those without a voice. Open your mouth, not for wine, but for the rights of the poor and needy.
Finally, you need to find an excellent wife!
Enclosed are my thoughts on the subject.

Your loving Mother

Scholars say that King Lemuel was a son of David (Solomon) and that Lemuel might have been a pet name given him by his mother (Bathsheba). His mother was concerned about the direction of his life, he took her advice to heart at least enough to preserve it for future generations, and it is still relevant for today.

A godly and loving mother wants her son to understand the importance of finding a good wife. She knows that this decision will set the course for his happiness and success. Proverbs 31:10-31 is a Hebrew acrostic poem meant to give specific virtues or qualities that define an excellent wife. The woman described is a figurative prototype of the qualities that embody the essence of feminine virtue. I see each of the following twenty one verses as illustrations of those virtues.

To paraphrase verse 10, "A woman of excellence is rare and hard to find. When you do discover her, treasure her because she is more costly than jewels. You will recognize her by the virtues she demonstrates." As we study the rest of this famous passage I will give what I believe are the virtues that God wants us to emulate and their amplification for each respective verse. I like to look at this passage in terms of principles so that we don't stumble on the cultural differences between our modern society and those living in ancient times. Each of these principle qualities could have many applications for today. Two of those qualities are responses from husbands and children that are the reward of an excellent wife.

The Proverbs 31 Woman—An Excellent Wife   171

Qualities of and Responses to An Excellent Wife

- 31:11 Loyal—Her husband counts on her loyalty and sees her as his greatest asset.

- 31:12 Supportive—Her husband knows that he can trust her to not undermine him.

- 31:13 Industrious—She likes to work and have something to show for it.

- 3:14 Innovative—She goes out of her way to find the best way to do things. She doesn't settle for the easy way.

- 3:15 Sacrificial—She deprives herself of sleep to serve others, and humbly tends to the needs of her household.

- 3:16 Visionary—She dreams of doing bigger and better things and carries out plans to completion by using her own resources.

- 3:17 Healthy—She is in good physical shape and is not frail or fat!

- 31:18 Vigilant—She appreciates the importance of all her responsibilities and is vigilant about protecting what is hers. She looks out for the interests of her family.

- 31:19 Skillful—She does not just dabble in this or that, she is accomplished in what she does. She doesn't hesitate to learn new skills!

- 31:20 Generous—She is giving and compassionate to those in need.

- 31:21 Confident—She earns her confidence by meeting her family's needs. No needless worrying.

- 31:22 Beautiful—She's a classy lady with good taste in

decorating and clothing. Regardless of natural endowments she develops a beautiful image and cultivates her home for her family.

- 31:23 Wife of a leader—he is inspired to be the leader of his family by the love and care of his wife. He is admired for his selection of an excellent wife. He gets the praise and glory for her service—as Christ does when He is served by His church.

- 31:24 Professional—She is efficient and good at doing business with others in her community (as homemaker, help mate, or business owner).

- 31:25 Faithful—her attitude is one of trust in God and his promises and no credence to naysayers.

- 31:26 Wise—She thinks before she speaks and offers wisdom and kind truth instead of just criticizing.

- 31:27 Tireless—She puts the needs of her family first and is not lazy or self indulgent.

- 31:28 Respected by her children—Her children see her value in their father's eyes. They respect her for her example. The daughters want to be like her, the sons want wives like her! They've learned about womanhood from her.

- 31:29 Revered—She is verbally praised and given credit for her work and accomplishments. She is respected by her children, loved by her husband, and appreciated by all.

- 31:30 Godly—It is her reverence for God that makes her beautiful in the eyes of her family. This is what wins her their appreciation.

- 31:31 Glorified—God will be glorified in her.

God's High Standards

God didn't choose an easy, breezy prototype for women. He set the bar very high; so high that some women shy away from this part of the Bible. Keep in mind that the picture is given of a woman who has spent a life time growing into these virtues. If a man wants a great Christian wife, Proverbs 31 is the profile. If a woman wants to have a husband who leads and cherishes her, these qualities are the key.

Just in case you were getting bored with your marriage, Proverbs 31 has certainly given us worthy aspirations. Just in case you ever grow weary in prayer, Proverbs 31 provides a sense of urgency for women who want the kind of leadership given by the virtuous woman's husband. To be more like her (remember, it's a lifelong pursuit!) for our families is a fulltime job!

Single Women of Excellence

Many single women are desirous of finding a wonderful Christian man. It may be challenging to keep your eyes open on one hand, and on the other hand maintain trust in God for your future. Please keep your priorities in check and don't let yourself become too fixated on the groom and the white gown! If it is God's plan for you to marry, He will bring events and people together in His own time.

Understanding that God desires womanly excellence from all women, even those not married, may help us to keep balanced. The virtues and qualities of an excellent wife are really those of an excellent woman! Try to see it as a woman's role to cultivate those virtues and God's job to bring the results—even the long awaited result of having a husband. Or the result of a life of purity and service to God. If married women would open their hearts and homes to single women they would have a renewed gratitude for their own husbands. A single woman usually has no one but herself for financial support; no one but herself to do chores and maintenance; no one but herself to please. Though this may appeal to some married women bent on complaining about the quality of their marriage, most single, divorced, and widowed women will tell you that being alone can get old. In the church we are often guilty of making everything about marriage and parenting to the exclusion of singles. Though we do it unintentionally, married women need to repent of the tendency to alienate our single sisters in Christ.

For the young singles, understand that since your childhood you have either been cultivating or neglecting the virtues needed to attract your desired husband. Don't expect that a man should be entranced merely by your smile and outer beauty, or settle for your undeveloped potential. You should have high character standards for the profile of your future husband. Ask God to help you become the kind of virtuous woman who can attract someone with high godly standards.

Here is a truth that Christian women need to pass on to their daughters in their early teen years: The wedding ceremony does not transform a woman into an excellent wife. Her training begins in the nursery and finds completion in the daily activities of sacrificing one's pride and vanity to the loving service of God and others. As those qualities develop, so may a godly man's attraction to her, regardless of her natural endowments. In much the reverse, a godly man may loose all attraction for a physically beautiful, but frivolous woman who isn't inclined to serve. A foolish man will be deceived, but a man who simply wants the best in this life will hold out for the virtuous woman. These are the truths that Lemuel's mom passed on to him.

To Be Glorified

Of all the virtuous woman's qualities, I think the most wonderful is also the most intimidating. In verse 31, "Give her the fruit of her hands, and let her works praise her in the gates." God will be glorified in this woman largely through her husband's praise of her when he meets with the other leaders of his community. He will value her and others will see her nurturing love in his confidence and delight. This should be the thing that we women fantasize about. Instead of dreaming of a better husband, or regretting our own less than perfect choices, why not dream about how to make the most of what we have? Let the fantasy consist of what God could do in your marriage if you were to treat your man as if he were the best husband on earth. How would that impact the way a woman relates to her husband? Live in a way that would inspire a good man to sing your praises.

When one thinks of glorifying God, do you see the connection with being a good wife? Each one of us will be judged for our own actions and attitudes, so we shouldn't seek to control what spouses and grown children do. But we should seek to do everything in our own spiritual and moral power to please and obey God. The Proverbs 31 woman does many things, but the most important ones relate to her husband and children. She brings glory to God by doing things that are humble and largely unnoticed by non family members. Her children thrive, her household is secure, and her husband is more successful due to her care of him.

Realistically, we may or may not be praised by husbands who are burdened with serious work concerns. Our children may not currently call us blessed as we vigilantly teach them manners and morals. There may or may not be many visible results seen by the world. But the amazing thing is that she will have a reward some day. One way or another, God will glorify the godly woman.

The Life Giver
The Proverbs 31 woman has a calling which is important to God. It may not always be appreciated by those she serves. It may not be understood by society. Even other Christian friends may not see the importance of a role that doesn't bring home a pay check. For all who see their role of humble service to family as the greatest call of a biblical woman there is great promise in Romans 8:30, "And those whom he predestined he also called, and those whom he called he also justified, and those whom he justified he also glorified." This promise is for all who humbly follow Christ.

This is the real goal, that our lives reflect the glory of God. That is what happens when you breastfeed your baby and relax about your figure for a season. Glorifying God is what's happening when one finds joy in playing on the floor with a toddler or reading books to your children of all ages. Pointing the way to God's glory is taking place when a mom teaches modesty to her daughters. You bring others into the glory of God when you encourage parents instead of criticizing needlessly. God is greatly glorified when mothers are physically there for their kids at the end of a school day and not just parenting via cell phones. God is glorified when a woman stays in an unfulfilling marriage for the sake of her children. God's promise is clear: if you are His child by faith, through Jesus he will see you glorified! As married women, our greatest arena for glorifying God is in the HOME!

The woman of excellence in Proverbs is full of enthusiasm and energy. She is not a mere drone or worker bee. This woman thrives on serving and ministry. She is energized by her relationship with God. It is her love for God which causes her to be committed to excellence in all that she does. She has a vision for her efforts. God's prototype is not about just getting things done. She cares how they are done. She has a vision of giving life and beauty to others through her deeds. Through all that she is and does, the Proverbs 31 woman is the essence of life giving and creativity. This is her inheritance from Eve. God created Eve and all of her sisters to be givers and nurturers of life. This must have been an appealing and beautiful thing to Adam who named his wife "Living." (cf. Gen. 3:20)

The Vision
Don't let a lesser fantasy of worldly success or romantic trysts ruin God's vision for you. Learn to develop your inner dreams and desires around the beautiful picture of the virtuous and excellent woman who glorifies God by serving others. Dream of becoming the kind of woman who will be respected by her children and loved by her husband (Prov. 31:8), knowing that God will make it possible if you obey him. One way for single women to be nurturers

is to strategize ways to help encourage parents and teens who may struggle in your church. Instead of just listening when friends start husband bashing, encourage those women to appreciate their husbands. Married women need to focus on ways to improve their husband's wives, not resenting men. If we surrender our hearts and minds to the transforming power of God's Word, then we will see a change in the way we think and live.

Would you rather have money, or happy and secure children? Are you after approval from society, or giving affection to your husband? Do you want to merely impress the people at your church or work place with your many deeds, or do you want to be a humble blessing in the home? Must you pursue all of your dreams now, or can you sacrifice those until your children have been well equipped to pursue theirs? With every question, the godly woman is compelled to choose the latter. The latter choice of happy children, well loved husband, and humble and sacrificial serving is the choice to glorify God. In so doing, the woman of God is glorified in Christ beyond what any selfish ambition could envision.

The Older Women
I believe the key to all this is found in Titus 2:1-5, "But as for you, teach what accords with sound doctrine. Older men are to be sober-minded, dignified, self-controlled, sound in faith, in love, and in steadfastness. Older women likewise are to be reverent in behavior, not slanderers or slaves to much wine. They are to teach what is good, and so train the young women to love their husbands and children, to be self-controlled, pure, working at home, kind, and submissive to their own husbands, that the word of God may not be reviled."

These are the Apostle Paul's instructions to older women. This passage assumes that it is the older women who are the experts in these matters. Not merely because they are older, but because they have been spending their own lives in the pursuit of biblical womanhood. Older women are not to be living self-focused, self-indulgent lives of frivolity. Of course, in our culture that is a choice that many make in various forms. Many women distance themselves from the realm of babies and small children as soon as their own children are in school. Plenty of women spend their days shopping and focusing on their own vanity instead of using their free time to minister and serve in their communities. Scores of women leave their neighborhoods and homes on a daily basis hoping to impact the world and earn income, overlooking the many ministry opportunities to reach out to other women and families. This is their right, but not the plan of God.

I am not saying that all women should be gardening and culinary aficionados. I am not condemning all professional pursuits or wage earning out side the home. Scripture does not, nor do I, teach that we should go back to the Middle Ages. In fact, many women wish they could be fulltime homemakers, or cut back to part time employment. Maybe in their cases their husbands don't value their domestic contributions as much as their earning potential. I fear, in more cases than not, women are too quick to discard the very great calling of the Proverbs 31 woman who freelanced from home. This commitment to the home arena is not possible for every wife and mother, but it is God's ideal. The Proverbs 31 woman is a woman of excellence whose example is not for the faint hearted or lax woman. Her greatest dreams and inspirations begin and thrive from home. She spends enough time and energy on her home and family to make her home a cherished haven!

For women who, for one reason or another, are not able to commit to this freelance nurturing from home lifestyle there is something better than cynicism and defeat. There is something better than disdain for what one cannot enjoy. There is prayer for spiritual discernment. There is study of Scripture to discover the aspects of biblical womanhood that one can pursue. There is the transforming power of God's Word as he helps women in all seasons of life to discover the joy of nurturing wherever God places us. There is the encouraging knowledge that Christian women are meant to be sisters in Christ, not competitors or rivals.

Spiritual Mothering
There is a current interest in mentoring in our secular and church culture. No doubt there is a place for different types of mentoring between women. But there is a biblically distinct role as leader and discipler for the mature godly woman. There are distinctives to which younger godly women should aspire. What Paul presents in Titus 2:3 is more akin to spiritual mothering than the usual idea of mentoring. He calls for godly older women to be models and teachers of womanly excellence. They are to assertively find ways to reach out to younger women and teach them the following: love their husbands and children, self-control, purity, domestic skills, kindness, and submission in marriage, and God's word. These are things that one must first understand from experience. These are ideas that are not taught in women's magazines.

Let the women who don't care for submission get their information from talk shows. Let the women who are angry at men whine to their friends. Let the mom who wants to rush through the early years of child rearing settle for parenting books. Personally, I prefer the guidance of older, godly women who have given their lives in humble service to home and community. We need the accountability of these women who have seen much and given sacrificially. We need to hear their testimonies. We need their friendship. It takes humility to listen to them. We need that most of all.

The Wise Woman
In Proverbs 31:24-25 we see a woman of healthy confidence and poise. She uses her time and resources wisely. She isn't one for sitting around and worrying about things. She controls the things she should be in control of and surrenders the rest to God. Her attitudes and actions reflect this. She can "laugh at the time to come." She has a sense of humor and can take risks. She radiates Jesus to those in her sphere of influence. She is probably a good friend. Younger women admire her. Even if it is not obvious to everyone she knows, she has something to offer because of the

work she has done to become confident and wise.

In Proverbs 31:26 she opens her mouth with wisdom. She speaks intentionally. She says what needs to be said. This takes a lifetime to cultivate! Some women need years of humble pie to control their tongue; some women need maturity to become braver with their words. Her intentions are kind, her words are wise.

The Bread of Idleness

Usually, when I think of idleness I think of physical laziness. In Proverbs 31:27 we are warned of another kind of idleness: idle nurturing. As women, we are gifted as nurturers. It is actually possible to use that ability for evil. One can nurture gossip, envy, strife, pride, and many other sinful behaviors. One can promote bad language, fault finding, and rebellion by a simple misuse of the tongue. The wise woman does not let her mind and tongue just wander in every conceivable direction. She avoids the following ingredients to the bread of idleness: gossip and talking about people in a way that is self-serving; deceptive words meant to hide ulterior motives; and critical words meant to undermine or harm another. Those are the verbal manifestations of folly. A reckless woman will meet with her own folly in the end!

The Proverbs 31 woman is not to be confused with proud, critical, competitive, and prying women who don't have true wisdom and friendship to offer. She is a woman of wisdom and kindness. She nurtures growth and love with her words.

"She looks well to the ways of her household." The woman who fears the Lord does not exploit people. She does good deeds for pure motives. She is not selfish in her efforts to please people. She takes care of her immediate family before trying to save the world.

The Present Mothers

As I study Scripture's call for women to be spiritual mothers to each other, I see two major obstacles to this vision: young women who are in their early years of parenting and marriage are often too proud to acknowledge the wisdom of their elders; and those elder women are less and less present in the lives of those young women. Think about it! Sooner or later a well intentioned young woman is going to need a word of encouragement or advice from a woman with more experience and maturity. Aside from one's relatives, the usual channels for anything more than a brief hello are at a Bible study, a daytime ministry/volunteer function, and in the neighborhood. The woman with grown children who is active in her neighborhood by offering hospitality; or volunteering in the community; or serving in women's ministries in her church is becoming rarer. Either these women feel the pressure to go into the work force fulltime, with little time for ministry outside of their own stressed homes, or they have given up on trying to be relevant to women and ministries in general who don't take them seriously.

In the event that young women in the varying stages of womanhood would be open to teaching and mothering from more mature women in their varying seasons of life, we Christian women are compelled by Proverbs 31 to be organized for such opportunities. Proverbs 31:26 says that the godly woman, "Opens her mouth with wisdom, and the teaching of kindness is on her tongue." In response to this verse there are two possible solutions to the obstacles mentioned above: Young Christian women need to be so in tune to the biblical vision for womanhood that they are more realistic and humble; and older Christian women need to put their confidence in God, model biblical womanhood, and start teaching it to women. Teaching and ministering along these distinctively Titus lines is often lacking in Bible studies. This is the meat of women's ministries which makes our lives and friendships meaningful substance, instead of fluff.

Lasting Beauty
King Lemuel's mother closes her poem to her son by saying, "Charm is deceitful, and beauty is vain, but a woman who fears the Lord is to be praised. Give her the fruit of her hands, and let

her works praise her in the gates." Surely, these are the words of a woman who has experienced the changing seasons of life. She has known the thrill of early womanhood; she has possessed enough physical beauty to attract a king; she has suffered her own share of mistakes and endured God's scorching discipline; she has been faithful to God and humbly worked with hands of repentance; she has learned to seek after God and his eternal pleasures; she has grown old and lost loved ones. Lemuel's mother had much wisdom for her son and for us.

Compared to reverence for God, some of the world's most prized accomplishments are futile and wasted. A woman's magnetic personality can be misleading. Even rare and exceptional beauty will not endure a lifetime. She might possess those external qualities, but they are not her assurance. She doesn't have to cling to them in desperation as the years of her life pale away. The drooping and aging of her physical appearance will be credited to her as the battle wounds of mothering and womanhood. Those signs of age will usher in a new era of insight and godliness to those who are seeking out her wisdom. It is the woman whose life reflects faithful reverence for God who will bring great honor and praise to herself and her family.

In Proverbs 31 God gives us a challenging and beautiful vision of a woman of excellence. The virtuous woman is our model for the many seasons of Christian womanhood. Her example is not something we were ever meant to pursue alone and isolated in our homes. It is also not a wise choice for us to curtail the pursuits of caring for husbands, inviting friends over, and making our homes havens of rest and beauty. There are plenty of ways for the woman of excellence to be relevant without ignoring domestic harmony. The wise woman does not expect to be paid in the currency of this world for her eternal pursuits. She delights in things that cannot be bought: love, affection, respect, admiration, free time, and hobbies.

If it was crucial thousands of years ago for one godly mother to teach her son the many attributes of a virtuous wife, isn't it equally vital today for us as Christian women to learn, model, and teach these principles to each other? Everywhere there are examples of older ladies who have quietly, faithfully, and beautifully been women of excellence. We need to affirm their value by respecting them and opening up to their wisdom. Let us run to our spiritual mothers and aspire to become the same for others. Women will be most satisfied when we give life to our families first and nurture nurturing in each other. May our homes be a haven for family and friends and become the number one arena for bringing glory to God.

Questions for Study and Discussion:

1. Based on the first nine verses of Proverbs 31, how would you describe Lemuel's mother? List a few traits implied by her words to her son.

2. The author of this study gave the principles or virtues illustrated in each verse (vss.10-31). Go through each of those verses listing a key principle, either from the author or one of your own.

3. Now, let's talk about application, or a modern day illustration of each principle. Think about and make a one by one list of how these principles would be played out in today's world. Good for group discussion.

4. What do you find most challenging or convicting about this woman? (hint: conviction sometimes comes in the form of annoyance!)

5. From Scripture, point out some of the personal benefits she receives from her sacrificial nurturing.

6. Talk about the paradox between the humble nurturing of the virtuous woman and the love and respect she receives from her family.

7. How will this woman be misunderstood by our world?

8. How can single women give life and nurture in the home, church, and community?

9. What do you make of the vision for spiritual mothering?

10. Hebrews 13:1-2; and 1 Peter 4:7-11 talk about the Christian art of hospitality. What are the various ways Christian women can facilitate hospitality primarily, but not only, in the home.

11. In 1 Peter 4:9-11 Peter talks about hospitality in the home as the arena for the use of spiritual gifts. How might the home arena free women to discover and develop those gifts for God's glory?

12. How important is it for a woman of excellence to learn new skills? What are some examples of branching out to learn new things and how it can make one a better servant.

13. Does it affect your view of growing to be a Proverbs 31 woman to know that Lemuel's mother was Bathsheba? Explain.

❦❦❦❦❦❦❦❦❦❦❦❦❦❦❦❦❦❦❦❦❦❦❦❦❦❦❦❦❦❦

HANNAH: A VISIONARY MOTHER

❦❦❦❦❦❦❦❦❦❦❦❦❦❦❦❦❦❦❦❦❦❦❦❦❦❦❦❦❦❦

Scripture Reference:
1 Samuel 1-3

God's Silence

In the days before Israel had a king, the people of God were ruled by judges and priests. The judges were called by God to deliver his people from oppression and paganism. Some were primarily military leaders, others were mainly prophets. The judges were necessary because of the unfaithfulness of God's people and his merciful rescue of them during intervals of self inflicted punishment. The book of Judges concludes with these sad words, "In those days there was no king in Israel. Everyone did what was right in his own eyes."

In I Samuel there is wide spread corruption among the temple priests. The never fully conquered pagan inhabitants of the land present many temptations for the Hebrews and their leaders. The priests exploited the faithful by taking the best portions of ritual sacrifices for themselves; by prostituting women for their own gratification and financial gain; and generally participating in pagan practices.

Two of the most corrupt priests of Israel are Hophni and Phinehas, sons of one of our study's main characters, the high priest Eli. He is referred to as having judged Israel for forty years in 1 Samuel 4:18. The sinful and corrupt behavior of Eli's sons was well known. He was aware of it, distressed by it, and completely ineffectual in stopping it. In fact the days of Eli are characterized by prophetic inactivity. The priests were meant to be the keepers of the temple or tabernacle (housed in tents) and ministers of truth and compassion to the Israelites. At best, Eli was mediocre in his calling.

One of the faithful Jewish families that would journey to the temple in Shiloh (twenty miles north of Jerusalem) to offer sacrifices and worship was the family of Elkanah from Ramah. We are told Elkanah's lineage and family dynamics in 1 Samuel 1:1-2. He has two wives: one Hannah who is barren and the other named Peninnah who had children. Polygamy was at variance with God's ideal for marriage but was allowed in the case of a childless first marriage as outlined in Deuteronomy 21:15-17. There were regulations stipulating fair inheritance rights to the children and the wives. The practice of polygamy caused great family strife as we will see. It was never God's intention for families.

Spiritual Darkness

Every year Elkanah would take his family to Shiloh to worship and sacrifice to the "Lord of Hosts." This picture of "Lord of Hosts" is that of a military figure, referring to God as the One who commands the angelic armies of heaven. This spiritual reality is in bold contrast to the corrupt state of affairs in the temple and the lives of the Jewish people at this time. Interestingly, Hophni and Phinehas, the notorious sons of Eli, were priests there. So we see the faithful, but faulty family coming to observe their faith with the aid of fraudulent priests. What a picture of spiritual darkness! What a dismal scene of malfunction! On the surface it may seem that God has departed from Israel.

To make matters worse, in an effort to show his love to Hannah, Elkanah favors her with a double portion (which was meant to be eaten) of the sacrifice, while giving Peninnah and her sons and daughters the correct amount. He loved Hannah deeply, even though she could not bear him children. To Peninnah this must have been a reminder of her lower status. Unfortunately, she could not rise above jealousy and be thankful for her children. She would use her success at childbearing as a way of provoking and abusing Hannah. She had no womanly compassion, just womanly contempt! If any family needed help, this family did. But instead they have Eli's corrupt sons for leadership.

We are told in 1 Samuel 1:17 that due to Peninnah's merciless provocation, Hannah wept and would not eat. Was she trying to show that she would not benefit from the double portion given by her husband? Was she simply too distressed to eat? Christian women willing to face their problems are wise to fast for a time of prayer and seeking after God. Introspection and prayer through crisis is more healthy and productive than eating to avoid the pain of life. The kind of overeating which is so common in our culture is a relatively new phenomenon. We should be quicker to take spiritual stock and face issues in our lives, and slower to put hand to mouth! When a woman is thrust into a crisis or has chronic marital issues and problems, she is best equipped to seek after God by eating less and spending more time in prayer, study, and exercise. She will allow herself to feel the full force of her emotions when she is alone with God. Those times alone with God will enable her to get it together for her family! She will eat on a schedule and find her sustenance in Christ.

Another point working for Hannah was her aloneness. There may well have been no mother, sister, or best friend whom she could trust or confide in. Sometimes we simply do not have what we need in those categories. Many of the greatest times of spiritual growth and victory are when God strips us of the leaders, friends, congregations, communities, and other important things that we rely on for comfort and strength. He says in essence, "I am all you have. Am I enough for you during this time?" These are times when a woman must turn to Scripture and prayer to see God's big picture. These are the times when a woman must make solitude her best friend.

I think Hannah was not just concerned about her own barrenness; she was concerned for her family. What kind of mother do you suppose Peninnah was? What kind of environment did her children live in? The situation for Hannah would have been distressing indeed! She went through this year after year. The last straw seems to have been when her well meaning husband says, "Hannah, why do you weep? And why do you not eat? And why is your heart sad? Am I not more to you than ten sons?" No, not by a long shot! In fact his love and favor was part of her problem!

Running to God
While preparing the food after the sacrifice, Peninnah once again berates and mocks Hannah. Hannah probably doesn't even want a single portion, much less a double portion. Who could eat under the weight of such anxiety? Doesn't Peninnah see how warped she is? Doesn't she care that her anger is destroying their family? One wonders if Elkanah thought Hannah was too thin from lack of food? Elkanah's lack of perception and Penninah's cruelty must have been maddening for Hannah as she endured one more year of torment at the hands of Peninnah.

It seems in 1:9 that Hannah could not take the antagonism any longer and surprises every one by leaving dinner abruptly and running to the tabernacle. Their temple may not be spotless in its leadership, but she wants to get as close to God as possible. Eli the priest is sitting by the doorpost of the temple of the Lord. Notice that Scripture points out that the temple is still the Lord's. God has a sovereign plan that transcends human failure. His plan is symbolized by the temple itself and the many rituals and sacrifices carried out there. To Hannah, the temple is a place of refuge.

In the temple Hannah pours out her distress to the Lord. Out of breath, with tears streaming down her face she stumbles to the floor of the altar. She pours out her turbulent emotions to God. At the doorpost of the temple, Eli the priest is sitting and sees Hannah. She is lost in her anguish and unconcerned about her appearance or surroundings. When was the last time you or someone you know became so visibly unrestrained in their brokenness in church? Rarely have I seen such a sight as Hannah must have presented to Eli. It was as if she were at the funeral of her child—the child she would never have. Hannah is truly broken. But brokenness is when we are free from pride, image, and self inhibitions. Brokenness is when we are most open to God's leading.

Because of our human pride we often recoil from the unfair demands put on us by life. If I haven't sinned, then why does it seem like I'm being punished? Because of pride we often assume that apart from personal sin we can expect him to facilitate our goals and requests. Why doesn't God answer my prayers? In those times we suffer from a woefully inadequate vision of God. He is in control even when our goals are thwarted. It is also pride on the part of any man or woman to assume that one's unfulfilled expectations are necessarily about one's sin, or need, or even about something God is trying to pin point. Sometimes those concerns are legitimate, but such spiritualized thoughts are often just another form of self focus. Occasionally God leaves us waiting simply because his timing is not what we expect; instead it is often a protracted and thorny mystery to us. True submission to God realizes that even unanswered prayers are not mostly about us. They are about what God is doing—and until he reveals himself to his servant, his business is his! I believe that as Hannah prayed in the temple she reached that point of surrender.

Hannah was very sensitive to the need for godly leadership for her self and her people. She could see her husband's family disaster first hand. One might question Elkanah's wisdom as a husband. Likely, he sees Hannah's barrenness as minor since he found an alternative means of fathering children. Hannah and everyone else are aware of the corruption of many of the priests, including the ones who served them. Perhaps she no longer wants a child just out of her own maternal longing. Given the circumstances, I think it is reasonable to believe that Hannah now wants a son who will become a righteous leader: Righteous like a Nazirite (referred to in her prayer of 1:11). A priest, but not a mere cleric like Eli. God lays it on Hannah's heart to ask Him for a son that would be a priest prophet. This is a woman who understands the need to hear a word from the Lord. And that word is just around the corner from where she prays.

I imagine that as Hannah pours out her distress to the Lord an unbearable thought comes to her as if straight from heaven: "Hannah, would you give me your son if you had one?" Hannah agonizes and wrestles with it. She concludes, "Yes, Lord, it would be better to see your glory again by giving up a son, than to never have one. This would be my one purpose. To have a son and give him to the Lord to be a holy man of God." So the woman with the heart of a mother, but the womb of a grave mouths the words, "O Lord of hosts, if you will indeed look on the affliction of your servant and remember me and not forget your servant, but will give to your servant a son, then I will give him to the Lord all the days of his life, and no razor shall touch his head."

It is as Hannah is making this sacrificial vow that Eli decides to interrupt her and confront her for the sin of drunkenness. Hannah's appearance during this great spiritual exertion must have been shocking for Eli to witness. She seems drunk to him because her lips move, but nothing coherent comes out of her mouth. She is an emotional wreck and perceptibly not in a normal state. Perhaps it has been a long time since Eli has seen such brokenness. When he wrongly corrects her she speaks up and says on her own behalf: "No, my lord, I am a woman troubled in spirit. I have drunk neither wine nor strong drink, but I have been pouring out my soul before the Lord. Do not regard your servant as a worthless woman, for all along I have been speaking out of my great anxiety and vexation." Broken though she may be, Hannah is still articulate and determined. Eli evidently sees the truth about Hannah, but he does not necessarily know the nature of her concern.

Eli's answer to Hannah is, "Go in peace, and the God of Israel grant your petition that you have made to him." It seems by Hannah's response she has taken encouragement from Eli: "Let your servant find favor in your eyes." Then she went away and ate, and her face was no longer sad. It is healthy to eat and enjoy food regularly! When Hannah and her family return to Ramah, she and Elkanah live as husband and wife. I believe Hannah fully expected God to grant her petition as indicated by her change of demeanor and behavior. I imagine she became a happier wife as well as physically intimate with her husband as a result of her encounter with God.

Hannah's Vision

I am struck by Hannah's remarkable sense of vision born out of heartbreak and suffering. Her words convey a vivid understanding of not only her own problems, but the predicament of her people. She seems to make a sacrificial vow because she knows a sacrifice is in order in the very environment in which temple sacrifices are treated flagrantly. Like all godly saints throughout history, Hannah has a sense of urgency, not just about her own suffering, but about the greater mess of the world as she knows it. Hers is a world of ineffectual leaders and their inferior offspring. Hers is a world of spiritual bankruptcy.

Men like Elkanah could focus on and solve the problem of needing physical heirs to property, but only God can raise up leadership. Only God creates visionary men and women. It is encouraging to understand from Hannah's life that God often uses women and their visionary gifts to form and encourage leaders. We women should never become too proud to lead the way in supportive roles and raising godly daughters and sons.

Hannah's Integrity

Is it any real consolation for her in knowing that Elkanah favors her over Peninnah? No, because it creates jealousy and vindictiveness in Peninnah. The second wife knows that she will always just be the mother and not the cherished wife. It says a lot about Hannah that she doesn't find satisfaction in being the favorite.

On a personal and national level, Hannah and her people are in a crisis of leadership. Eli is a good man, but he is polarized by the outrageous behavior of his priest sons—sons who have been allowed to digress to the point of defiling sacrifices and sexual immorality. They would not listen to their father. It is said that he was not hard enough on them.

The Lord Remembered Her

We know from 1 Samuel 1:19 that the family arose the next morning and worshipped before the Lord, then returned to their house at Ramah. The text tells us that Elkanah knew Hannah his wife, and the Lord remembered her. She later conceived and bore a son and called his name Samuel, because "I have asked of him from the Lord." Samuel literally means "heard of God." There is a message in this: God hears and speaks to those whose hearts are fully surrendered to him.

God's Sovereignty in the Sin of Man

It is also interesting to note that Elkanah agrees to the vow made by Hannah. How is it that this man is willing to give up his only son by the woman he loves so much? According to the laws of Moses in Numbers 30:10, a husband can nullify the vow of his wife. I speculate that the sons Elkanah had with Peninnah might have made it endurable for him to support Hannah's vow. Could it be that the Lord allows bad things into our lives to orchestrate something that will bring him tremendous glory later? Even though we don't have to deal with the same exact things as Hannah, the principle is about God's sovereignty. God will not be stopped from accomplishing his will. He wanted Hannah's son and brought circumstances to this point!

We also cannot overlook the softening effect of a submissive wife. Elkanah might have been very moved to obey God out of respect for his wife's renewed love for him.

Like Hannah, in our own lives we may have to live with the consequences of sin and bad choices thrust on us by others. We may find ourselves in a time of spiritual darkness and silence from God. Lest we forget that God is in control, His word is infused with flashes of his sovereign power and grace. One such "God flash" is found in 1 Samuel 2:25-26 when Eli confronts his sons for their sin and corruption as leaders: "But they would not listen to the voice of their father, for it was the will of the Lord to put them to death." We may prefer to believe that every person is absolutely responsible for their own actions and sins. But on a deeper level we must understand the far reaching control of God. He is weaving a plan which may involve suffering for now, but will result in great glory for him and those who obey him. Those who refuse to submit to God may not have as much control of their lives as they take for granted! Bad leaders are ultimately not a problem for God. His power and mercy will always provide a steady supply of leaders who will emerge when he calls. One such leader would be Samuel as we see in verse 26, "Now the young man Samuel continued to grow both in stature and favor with the Lord and also with man.

"Hannah Did Not Go Up"
The next year when Elkanah and all his house went to offer the yearly sacrifice and to pay his vow (we don't know the nature of the vow), Hannah did not go up. She told Elkanah in 1:22, "As soon as the child is weaned, I will bring him, so that he may appear in the presence of the Lord and dwell there forever." Elkanah's response: "Do what seems best to you; wait until you have weaned him; only, may the Lord establish his word." We don't know if this was the first time Hannah explained her vow to Elkanah or if she was just reiterating her plans for the boy. The most important thing is that Elkanah allows Hannah to keep what for both of them would be a sacrificial vow. Hannah's renewed love for her husband may also have gone a long way in motivating him to honor her vow.

According to verse 4 Hannah did take the boy with her later along with a three year old bull to be sacrificed. Perhaps the bull was the same age as the boy. Due to the required sacrifice of a bull, which was very costly, those who took the Nazirite vow were from well-off families. The age of three would have been a common age then for weaning. It also would have been enough time for a mother to be able to teach basic lessons of love and respect for authority.

"He is Lent to the Lord"

So, when Samuel is about three years old, his mother and father take him to the house of the Lord at Shiloh and they take him to Eli. There is something exhilarating for Hannah in the scene of :6 when she says to Eli, "Oh, my lord! As you live my lord, I am the woman who was standing here in your presence, praying to the Lord. For this child I prayed, and the Lord has granted me my petition that I made to him. Therefore I have lent him to the Lord. As long as he lives, he is lent to the Lord." And he, Eli, worshipped the Lord there. The choice of words, "lent to the Lord," is significant. Hannah would still mother the boy by sewing for him and visiting him. She and Elkanah don't disown him. They are dedicating him to service in the temple.

Can you imagine the incredulity of Eli to realize that the attractive and happy woman with a child in her arms is the one whom he had seen behaving like an emotional wreck more than three years earlier? How would Eli register the sacrificial act taking place before his eyes? With great meekness. What were the chances that anyone would give him, a man who had failed with his own sons, custody of their precious answer to prayer? The mother in essence trusts him to raise the child as a Nazirite, one vowed to the strictest and holiest of lives. Not just for a few years, but for as long as he lives. Could it be that this child will be his recovery? Could this child be a deliverer for their people?

Notice that ever since Hannah made her petition to the Lord years earlier there has been no mention of Peninnah. She has faded into the background. Perhaps she was shamed by Hannah's selfless vow. In the big scheme of things Peninnah, Hannah's rival, does not matter. Just let that sink in. The small minded people who make life wretched for those who innocently threaten their status quo will meet their own folly in the end. This folly is detailed in

Hannah—A Visionary Mother

Hannah's prayer which was perhaps given before the assembly.

Hannah's Prayer of I Samuel
On that day of presenting Samuel over to the Lord, a very different woman from the one who petitioned the Lord for him, stood before the assembly to pray a prayer of victory. This woman was, I believe, beautiful with her son in her arms and the radiance of the exalted Lord in her countenance. Here is a paraphrase of I Samuel 2:1-10 of the prayer she would have stood to say:

> "My heart takes such joy and pleasure in the Lord! In Him is the source of my strength and vindication! Because of the Lord I can mock my enemies. Lord, your salvation gives me great rejoicing!
> No one compares to the holy, strong, and all knowing God.
> He knows all and judges all
> The mighty are really weak
> The feeble are actually strong
> Those who are full and proud will someday beg for bread.
> The hungry are now full
> The barren woman is a busy fulfilled mother
> She who has many sons has nothing to be proud of
> It is the Lord who is sovereign over life and death!
> He controls human wealth and position
> He decides the success and course of nations, rulers, and peoples, and even the pillars of the earth
> He is faithful and loyal to his faithful, but with out mercy to those who are wicked.
> Might won't save anyone!
> God is going to be the obvious winner of the war against his adversaries.
> He will judge
> He will give strength to his king
> He will exalt the power of his anointed"

No matter how one paraphrases Hannah's prayer the theme is simple: Full confidence and satisfaction in God's sovereignty. He is the Lord of hosts as mentioned early on in 1:3. His heavenly armies are already winning the battle. He controls human events and even looks out for the victims of evil. He has compassion for a barren woman like Hannah and does not bless women like Peninnah, even though she may be very fertile! And at the end of her prayer Hannah is very prescient: God has a king in mind that Israel knows nothing of yet! He has an anointed (also referring to the future Messiah?) whom no one on earth can direct!

All is resolved for Hannah and her family as 2:11 poignantly conveys: "Then Elkanah went home to Ramah. And the boy ministered to the Lord in the presence of Eli the priest."

Samuel is Safe in God's Sovereignty
Hannah must have prayed diligently for Samuel. Eli was not evil like his sons, but he was not an effective disciplinarian. When he rebuked his worthless sons in 1 Samuel 2:22 they were not receptive. God warned Eli through another prophet in verse 27 that he would put to death Eli's sons. This is in stark contrast to verse 26 which says, "Now the young man Samuel continued to grow both in stature and in favor with the Lord and also with man." In some ways Eli had a second chance with Samuel, but it was the hand of God directing his life that protected the boy. A strong focal point of Samuel's life would have been the yearly visits with his mother who made him a special robe. In verse 2:20 Eli blesses Elkanah and his wife by saying, "May the Lord give you children by this woman for the petition she asked of the Lord." We are told that the Lord did visit Hannah and gave her three sons and two daughters.

Samuel continued to grow in God's favor. As recorded in chapter 3 he was very distinctly called by God. He became the last judge of Israel; a priest, prophet, and leader to the people of Israel. He anointed the first king of Israel, Saul. He was saddened when Saul fell from the Lord and departed from his presence. Samuel also anointed David. In all of Israel's history, Samuel is considered one of the bright spots of hope and integrity. Certainly, Hannah herself would have said that no suffering at the hands of her rival was too much to endure for seeing the Lord of hosts victoriously at work!

May we post modern women seize Hannah's high vision of God's sovereignty and approach every thing we do or hope to be as a vehicle for his glory and work, trusting the Lord of hosts with our families. May we love and raise our children as treasures from the Lord and offered up for his glory!

Questions for Study and Discussion:

1. What is the significance of barrenness for women, regardless of the era of history in which we live?

2. In verse 3 God is called "the Lord of hosts" in the English Standard Version. Go through chapters 1 and 2 to find how many times this title is given. What is its importance?

3. Based on 1:1-8 what kind of leader would you say Elkanah is? (List good points and bad)

4. What do you speculate is the importance of Hannah's weeping and not eating in 1:1-8? How is this similar to and/or different from what we call "depression"?

5. How do you think you, or Hannah, would feel after hearing Elkanah's words of comfort in 1:8?

6. What are some possible reasons for God giving us a quote from Elkanah? What might it tell us about her situation?

7. In 1:10 Hannah is extremely distressed. It is in this distress that she makes a very serious vow. Using one word, please describe the nature of her prayer.

8. What part does surrender play when we are disappointed by life?

9. Hannah's supreme sacrifice comes at a time when her people were enduring corrupt leadership. From I Samuel 13:12-17; 22-25 what were the problems with Eli's sons?

10. How does Hannah inspire you as a mother?

10

ABIGAIL: PERCEPTIVE AND BEAUTIFUL MESSENGER

Scripture Reference:
1 Samuel 25

Abigail possessed the two traits most desired by women everywhere: beauty and intelligence. Her beauty was apparent to David and presumably everyone around her. Her intelligence was the kind that perceives people and issues quickly and takes the wisest course of action. Combined, these two qualities saved her household, mortified her husband, and won the heart of a king.

The Making of A King

Our story opens with a reference to the death of the great prophet and judge Samuel. This is significant for David and the nation of Israel. Samuel was a bridge between the judges and the kings. He was Saul and David's mentor and the spiritual leader of Israel. When the first king of Israel, Saul, was rejected by the Lord, Samuel was told by God to anoint one of the sons of Jesse. Samuel followed God's leading and anointed the youngest of Jesse's sons, David. Even though God was displeased with Saul, he allowed him to live and continue ruling Israel for many years. Saul's volatile emotions towards David vacillated between needy affection for the one whom he knows God now favors, and ruthless paranoia against his more popular successor. Earlier (1 Samuel 16) in his relationship with Saul, David was called upon to soothe the king's troubled spirit with the lyre, a stringed instrument. Later he was hailed as a hero of the people for standing up and using a slingshot to slay the Philistine Goliath. Saul kept David in close proximity allowing a bond to form between him and his son Jonathon (I Samuel 18). Saul also gave his daughter Michel in marriage to David to ensnare him, but later gave her to another man (1 Samuel 25:44) to spite David.

David's faith in God, bravery in battle, and anointing from God was known throughout Israel and other regions. The people of God were disillusioned with Saul and looking for David to replace him. Saul's resentment grew when he heard the women celebrate the new hero with songs of praise: "Saul has struck down his thousands, and David his ten thousands."

The jealousy and greed of Saul reached the point of David fearing for his life. For years, David fled Saul's efforts to kill him or have him killed. David would hide in neighboring countries and even place his parents in the care of the Moabites (1 Sam. 22:4) for safe haven. He would build a stronghold in a wilderness hideout with his men and garner strength for the next battle against Saul. On one occasion in 1 Samuel 24 David is hiding in a cave when Saul enters the cave to relieve himself. He does not know that David and his men are sitting in the innermost part of the cave. David's men encourage him to take the life of Saul, but David merely cuts off a corner of Saul's robe without Saul knowing it! David explains to his men, "The Lord forbid that I should do this thing to my lord, the Lord's anointed, to put out my hand against him, seeing he is the Lord's anointed." With these words David persuades his men not to attack Saul. Saul left the cave without a clue of his audience.

Afterward, David comes out of the cave, and calls after Saul saying, "My lord the king!" David actually pays homage to the king by bowing to him and exclaiming, "Why do you listen to the words of men who say, 'Behold, David seeks your harm'? Behold, this day your eyes have seen how the Lord gave you today into my hand in the cave. And some told me to kill you, but I spared you...." David goes on to explain that he would never put out his hand against the Lord's anointed. He shows Saul the cut-off piece

Abigail—Perceptive and Beautiful Messenger

of his robe and declares, "May the Lord therefore be judge and give sentence between me and you, and see to it and plead my cause and deliver me from your hand."

David has a strong sense of judicial conscience. Saul's treatment toward him is unjust and evil and should not be overlooked. This is juxtaposed against his sense of God's sovereign power. When God wants to make him the ruler of Israel, he will deliver him from Saul and David will not have to take matters into his own hand. Saul is convicted with guilt and remorse by David's returning good for evil. He knows he has continually wronged David and promises not to harm him. But David knows that Saul's repentant mood won't last long, so "David and his men went up to the stronghold" (I Sam. 4:).

Nabal's Dishonesty and Greed

According to 1 Samuel 23:13 David has about six hundred men (as opposed to Saul's three thousand in the previously mentioned encounter) who hideout with him in their wilderness stronghold. These mountains and caves are splendid places for David and his men to hide, as well as bandits and criminals. So David and his men act as security and protection for sheepherders and farmers in the region in hopes of payment in food and provisions. They have been protecting the flocks of a certain man named Nabal. When sheep shearing time comes, a time of hospitality and celebrating, they have to ask for payment from Nabal. The name Nabal means fool. He has a reputation for being harsh and badly behaved. But he has a wife named Abigail, and she is known for her beauty and discernment.

So David sends ten young men to Carmel to speak to Nabal by greeting him politely, reminding him of the work they have done for him, and asking for either an invitation to the feast or at least some leftovers. The messengers obey David and come back with this reply from Nabal: "Who is David? Who is the son of Jesse? There are many servants these days who are breaking away from their masters. Shall I take my bread and my water and my meat that I have killed for my shearers and give it to men who come from I do not know where?" That is, Nabal accuses the men of being imposters. He implies that David, whoever he is, is of no importance to him even if they are who they say. He adds insult to injury by saying he doesn't owe them anything! Nabal has picked the wrong person to defraud! His answer is indicative of his character. Perhaps his treatment of David is also reflective of his political loyalties.

David says to his men, "Every man strap on his sword!" According to 1 Samuel 25:13 David and his men put on their swords and prepare to fight. About four hundred go up with David and two hundred remain with the baggage. As far as David is concerned, Nabal is a dead man. He will give to Nabal a taste of his own folly. But something happens to change the course of events.

Abigail's Brave Interception

A servant of Nabal's finds Abigail and tells her about the incident of Nabal railing at the messengers from David. He tells her in verses 14 through 16 of the goodness, efficiency, and bravery of David's men when they were under their protection by day and night. The servant is not just upset, or expecting Abigail to save her own neck. In verse 17 the servant says to Abigail, "Now therefore know this and consider what you should do, for harm is determined against our master and against all his house, and he is such a worthless man that one cannot speak to him." In other words—what do we do? You are the only one who can tell us what to do!

When one reads I Samuel 25, it is clear that the servant who goes to Abigail expects something wise from her. The servant is concerned about the injustice of his master and the welfare of his people. He seems to know he can trust Abigail to listen. He seems to have a high expectation of her capabilities.

Abigail does not disappoint us in this regard. She makes haste and starts packing gifts for David from her pantry. There must also have been lots of rapid bread baking as well! She loads up donkeys with food provisions that would blow away any ordinary family's grocery budget for the year! Her offerings include: two hundred loaves of bread, two skins of wine, one hundred clusters of raisins, two hundred cakes of figs, five seahs of grain, and five sheep already prepared, and the donkeys on which the provisions are packed! All of this from a household which is in the midst of celebrating a harvest in shearing time! I wonder if Nabal's wife decided that all the food meant for Nabal's partying would be better used to save their lives! Abigail orders her servants to ride in front of her, presumably to hurry them along and keep her husband from intervening, while she comes along behind them.

The Higher Mission
Since shearing time is a time of celebration, let us imagine that Abigail is wearing one of her finest linen gowns, perhaps something in sky blue with a silver belt showing off her trim waist. As Abigail saw David coming toward her with his army of incensed men, what was she thinking and feeling? Was she trembling with fear for her life? Was she praying for the right words? I think she was thinking about all the songs and legends she had heard about David and his bravery. If anyone was capable of annihilating her household it would be the daring David. She possibly asked the Lord to help her bring out the best in this man—a man she surmised to be God's anointed. We can guess what Abigail was thinking by what she did and said when she met with him. Certainly, David was not expecting to come across a beautiful woman who appealed to his nobler self!

In verse 1, as David was just around the bend from Abigail, he declared to his men, "Surely in vain have I guarded all that this fellow has in the wilderness, so that nothing was missed of all that belonged to him, and he has returned me evil for good. God do so to the enemies of David and more also, if by morning I leave so much as one male of all who belong to him." David was thinking about his righteous indignation and killing, loads of killing! I believe Abigail was thinking of stopping the bloodshed over such a foolish and hollow man as Nabal. She had to persuade David of two things: Nabal's irrelevance; and David's higher mission from God.

"On Me Alone"

When David first saw Abigail she was riding under the cover of the mountain. At first sight of David, Abigail hurried down off her donkey and fell before David on her face and bowed to the ground. She fell at his feet and said, "On me alone, my lord, be the guilt. Please let your servant speak in your ears, and hear the words of your servant."

There is so much to learn from this woman's plea, that it should be read in its entirety. Notice the simultaneous sense of respect and urgency in Abigail's words and actions. She bows and pays homage to David to show respect for his God-given, if not humanly acknowledged, authority. She completely disarms him by taking blame for the muddle of inhospitality. She then uses the most humble of words to refer to herself ("your servant") and the most respectful of words ("my lord") to refer to David. Also notice, that Abigail never refers to David directly by name. Her explanation, advice, and plea are completely non-directive. There is nothing shrill, bossy, threatening or combative in her language or demeanor.

Then in verse 5 Abigail takes a tack that should never have to be taken by a wife: she points out the foolishness of her husband. In this case, such candor is necessary and obviously true. With the words, "Let not my lord regard this worthless follow, Nabal, for as his name is, so is he," Abigail seems rather detached from her husband and speaks in a way that identifies more with David. Her husband is not a man who deserves honor and now is not the time for his wife to pretend otherwise! But she humbly takes the blame for the way David and his men have been treated so inhospitably. In spite of her husband's rudeness, she plays the part of the gracious hostess.

Abigail "Gets" It!

Abigail's words in 25:26 reveal that she is spiritually incisive. She knows something of David (unlike Nabal who was ignorant or at least claimed ignorance regarding David) and has insight about him. Here she is, needing to pacify an army intent on killing every male of her household; and yet she tells the leader of that army what he needs to know about his own turbulent calling from God! This is a woman with incredibly expansive insight. With these words she demonstrates that this life threatening incident for her is really about something else: "Now then, my lord, as the Lord lives, because the Lord has restrained you from bloodguilt and from saving with your own hand, now then let your enemies and those who seek to do evil to my lord be as Nabal." In other words, "You know how worthless Nabal is; let all your enemies be as irrelevant to you as he."

Have you ever had interactions with a strong Christian who listens well and yet doesn't need a lot of explanation about a concern you share with them? Abigail was one such person. She's married to a difficult man. She knows what it is to suffer and deal with private pains and frustrations. She may have been sold into marriage to Nabal because of his wealth. She knows how to take responsibility for her own purpose and happiness in life, because clearly her husband doesn't care about anyone else's welfare. She lives in a day when women were powerless to leave an abusive man. Can you imagine a more challenging or effective school for learning to be empathetic? Can you conceive of a more practical means for one to develop the gift of wisdom? If you are living a life of intense emotional demand maybe God is preparing you for a ministry which requires great discernment. If you have been ministered to by such a compassionate and discerning person, appreciate the unseen anguish that may have been part of their training. Without a doubt, Abigail was gifted at "getting it" when discernment was called for.

Non-Directive Counsel

Then in 25:27-31 Abigail presents by implication the course that David ought to pursue: "And now let this present [the food provisions] that your servant has brought to my lord be given to the young men who follow my lord. Please forgive the trespass of your servant. For the Lord will certainly make my lord a sure house, because my lord is fighting the battles of the Lord, and evil shall not be found in you so long as you live. If men rise up to pursue you and to seek your life, the life of my lord shall be bound in the bundle of the living in the care of the Lord your God. And the lives of your enemies he shall sling out as from the hollow of a sling. And when the Lord has done to my lord according to all the good that he has spoken concerning you and has appointed you prince over Israel, my lord shall have no cause of grief or pangs of conscience for having shed blood without cause or for my lord taking vengeance himself. And when the Lord has dealt well with my lord, then remember your servant."

David must have been stunned from the moment he saw this beautiful woman, laden with gifts of food, dismounting her donkey and making her apologies. She takes the blame for her foolish husband's behavior. She frankly acknowledges Nabal's foolishness and puts it in perspective for David: Nabal is a worthless fellow not worth shedding blood over. He is even less important than all of your other enemies from whom God has saved you. Abigail reminds David that his battles are of the Lord, and he doesn't need to take vengeance himself. God will establish his throne. His promises are worth the wait!

Had rumors spread concerning David's pass on killing Saul in the cave? Wouldn't a woman as astute and spiritually aware as Abigail have known of David's purposes for camping out in the wilderness? Indeed, the very raw sense of righteous indignation present in David when wronged by Nabal is the same reaction he worked hard to stifle when dealt evil from the hand of Saul. The freshly insulted future king would need to be reminded by a woman, a very beautiful and articulate one, of God's providence.

God used Abigail's decisive actions, humble attitude, and big picture discernment to inspire David to that previous level of self control.

"Blessed Be You"

In verses 32 through 35 we see a grateful David. He was blessed by Abigail's swiftness and vision. She has reminded him of his purpose and kept him from being distracted by her worthless husband's sin. It is not Nabal who matters, but David's future role as king. Perhaps with the death of Samuel David needed to be reminded of the big picture.

Girded up for battle, with four hundred battle ready men at his back, David said to Abigail, "Blessed be the Lord, the God of Israel, who sent you this day to meet me! Blessed be your discretion, and blessed be you who have kept me this day from bloodguilt and from avenging myself with my own hand! For as surely as the Lord the God of Israel lives, who has restrained me from hurting you, unless you had hurried and come to meet me, truly by morning there would not have been left to Nabal so much as one male." Then David "received from her hand" all the provisions Abigail had brought. And he said to her, "Go up in peace to your house. See, I have obeyed your voice, and I have granted your petition."

Abigail Came to Nabal

I speculate this reprieve for Abigail would have been bitter sweet. Now she must go home to her shameful husband. She will have to explain recent events to him and suffer the consequences. One of the reasons for her bravery in going to David might have been that she could better anticipate fairness from her husband's enemy than from her husband! But her courage does not leave her as she returns to her house. She comes to Nabal and finds him holding a feast in his house, like the feast of a king. He's drunk according to verse 36 so she tells him nothing until the morning light. You cannot reason with a drunk!

Nabal had been feasting like a king—though he insulted God's anointed. He was making merry and celebrating his own success at tricking David and taking advantage of his flight from Saul.

In verse 37 we are told that, "In the morning, when the wine had gone out of Nabal, his wife told him these things, and his heart died within him, and he became as a stone. And about ten days later the Lord struck Nabal, and he died." Abigail's actions and David's near retaliation were a complete mockery of Nabal. He was not worthy of David or his valiant men; he was not worthy of Abigail; he was not worth shedding blood over. The realization that he had been bested by his enemy was literally mortifying for Nabal.

"Remember Your Servant"
When David received news of Nabal's death he sees it as vindication for the insult received at his hands. He reflected on the way he was kept from wrongdoing and said, "The Lord has returned the evil of Nabal on his own head." He then sent messengers to speak to Abigail and bring her back to be his wife. As she had requested, he remembered "his servant," a "servant" who helped him to rule his own passions.

When Abigail was greeted by the servants of David she responded with gratitude and humility: "Behold, your handmaid is a servant to wash the feet of the servants of my lord." Obviously complimented and pleased to go with them, she "hurried and rose and mounted a donkey, and her five young women attended her. She followed the messengers of David and became his wife."

She was remembered by David. He would give her the love and protection every woman desires. Yet the romance is a sub theme. God does not end the story with a perfect marriage. In verse 43 David also took another wife named Ahinoam of Jezreel. David had already been married to Michel, Saul's daughter who was taken back and given to another man. Perhaps marriage to David under any circumstances would be an improvement for Abigail. Sadly, polygamy was not uncommon among God's people and families were sorely troubled by its hazards. But it is crucial to note that God's realism is starkly displayed in his Word. His saints were not and are not flawless men and women. This account reveals how human David the king, prophet, artist, and visionary really was. God's Word was not written by people who contrived self serving fables. Every narrative, story, account, and proverb, leads us not to man and his importance but to God and His big picture of using blemished people to bring glory to himself.

Romance Revisited
Abigail was used by God to lead David back to God's vision for him. The romantic in me thinks he loved her at first sight and knew she would be a wonderful wife. She was used greatly and then humbly went back to a semi-ordinary life of raising a son. She bore David a son named Chileab. God is using each of us in ways that we may not understand or be appreciated for yet.

When Abigail told David that he would be "bound in the bundle of the living in the care of the Lord" when men tried to destroy him; she was reminding him of something that is true for all believers today as well as then. Our lives, families, careers, and ministries belong to God. If we are consecrated in service to God, then he will either protect us from evil for his glory, or allow calamity to befall us for his glory. For believers in Jesus our position is the same as David, we can trust the Lord to bring about his purposes. If we are fighting "the battles of the Lord" then he will give us victory in the manner in which he chooses. The realist in me finds comfort in knowing that God is in control, no matter how the romance turns out!

The life of Abigail is a real life drama, consisting of much more than romance. She was married to a "harsh and badly behaved" man. His name meant "fool" and he lived up to it. Yet she was somehow strong when faced with a crisis. She was attuned to the truth of her own situation and not afraid to face conflict. She knew when to be blunt and when to be less direct. She was faithful to her husband, but did not turn a blind eye to his sinfulness. She was submissive, but not a doormat. She demonstrated bravery and took risks to defend others. She was a prepared housewife and knew the loyalty and respect of trusted servants. Abigail was physically beautiful, and used her beauty for God's glory. She was perceptive about matters that not everyone at that time comprehended. She was humble, but not timid. She was articulate, but not mouthy. She was everything we as women today could hope to be. She was chosen by a dashing king. Yes, a romance, but a great deal more.

Questions for Study and Discussion:

1. In 1Samuel 25:3 we are told crucial details about Nabal and Abigail. Why do you think we are told about Abigail's beauty and intelligence?

2. How would you characterize Nabal's response in verses 10-11?

3. How would you characterize David's reaction in verse 13? Explain.

4. What are some observations we might surmise about Nabal and Abigail based on the words of the servant in verses 14-17?

5. What do Abigail's actions and words in verses 18-20 suggest about her as a woman?

6. In verses 32-35 we have David's grateful response to Abigail. Based on his words, how has his view of the situation evolved?

7. What does verse 36 indicate about Abigail's character?

8. Based on verse 39 how does David understand the death of Nabal?

9. Based on verses 40-42 how does Abigail respond to David's proposal?

10. Pertaining to verses 43-44 the author of the study talked about God's realistic presentation of people and events in the Bible. Please describe and discuss which aspects of this narrative are an inspiring romance, and which ones are a warning, and which are just a true telling of occurrences.

11. In verse 5 Abigail confirms an unpleasant truth about her husband. How might this be reconciled to Ephesians 5:-33?

12. What is the spiritual application of I Samuel 25 for women today in regards to communication between men and women? What are some specific things we can learn from Abigail's communication style and discernment?

13. Give specific examples from Scripture of how Abigail was supportive and submissive to David as a leader.

14. List Abigail's character qualities from 1 Samuel 25.

11

PRISCILLA: A WOMAN'S DRIVE FOR MINISTRY

Scripture references naming Priscilla:
Acts 18:2... "Aquila with his wife Priscilla"
Acts 18:18... "Paul took with him Priscilla and Aquila"
Romans 16:3... "Prisca and Aquila, my fellow workers in Christ Jesus"
1 Corinthians 16:19... "Aquila and Prisca, together with the church in their house"
2 Timothy 4:19... "Greet Prisca and Aquila"

Paul's Drive for Ministry

Our study begins in the book of Acts, authored by the great physician Luke who at times traveled with Paul on his missionary journeys. In Acts 17 the Apostle Paul is in Athens, waiting for his fellow missionaries Silas and Timothy. While waiting for them "his spirit was provoked within him as he saw that the city was full of idols." He is disgusted and troubled by the rampant immorality and idol worship. Paul reasoned with the Jews in the synagogues, and dialogued with devout persons he met, and preached in the market place to whoever was there everyday. Some of the Stoic and Epicurean philosophers also conversed with Paul, baffled by his talk about "strange and foreign divinities." Nothing in the Greek religious pantheon could weigh against the teachings of Jesus and the resurrection! So they reacted to the truth by taking hold of him and bringing him to the Areopagus, or the venerable council in charge of religious and educational matters in Athens which met outside the city on Mars Hill. They demanded that Paul explain what seemed to them a new teaching. According to Acts 17:21 all the locals would spend their time in "nothing except telling or hearing something new". But Paul had the advantage of knowing and appreciating something of their history. Make no mistake about it: the Apostle was no fan of their culture. He would use his knowledge to remind them of something the city fathers and populace had forgotten.

In his famous sermon to the esteemed leaders and intellectuals of Athens Paul seizes on something in their culture that points the way to God. He shows them, through their own history and literature that they are actually digressing from truth in their frenzied search for something new. If they will just look to the altar inscribed "to the unknown god" they will see how far they have strayed from their teacher Socrates. They will see how they have forsaken their great hero Pericles who erected altars to Socrates' belief in an unknown god. This reference would have been understood by the locals as the unknown god whom Socrates said could not be created or seen by man—that their own pantheistic religions only fall short of capturing the true Deity who chooses to elude man and his corruption. As seen Paul is a master at knowing his audience. This is an opportunity for which he is prepared as he further demonstrates by quoting two of their popular poets, Epimenides of Crete and Aratus.

Paul's brilliant declaration is simply that the "unknown god" of their past yearning is now revealed in the person of Jesus Christ. God has proven the power of his Son and given assurance to all by raising him from the dead. "The times of ignorance God overlooked," said Paul, "but now he commands people everywhere to repent." In other words, "Your national heroes were on to something, but now you can actually know God. You need to know him and repent of your sinful pride!" This message is used by many today as a model for reaching the unchurched. What was the fruit of this message?

The teaching of Christ's resurrection was mocked by some. Others inquired further. When Paul left some joined him and believed. Among them were Dionysius the Areopagite (a member of the council of philosophers) and a woman named Damaris and others with them. After this Paul went to Corinth, the Hellenistic capital of sin and carnal pleasure. Paul's drive for ministry was led by the Holy Spirit. It is believed that Paul never planted a church in Athens.

Divine Appointment
In Corinth Paul finds a Jewish man named Aquila who along with his wife Priscilla has recently come from Rome. This is due to the banishment of Jews from Rome by the Emperor Claudius in 49 or 50 A.D. Perhaps Paul met this man in a local synagogue. It seems he was invited to the man's home where he started a friendship with both Aquila and Priscilla. Paul was probably thrilled to discover that they shared the same trade of tentmaking. In Acts 18:1-4 we are told that Paul stayed with them and worked with them. In his free time he reasoned in the synagogue every Sabbath and tried to persuade Jews and Greeks. It seems that culturally Hellenized Jews attended the same synagogues as those who were separatists like the Pharisees. By their Greek names it is likely that Aquila and Priscilla were of the culturally Greek Jews who were more common in cities outside of Palestine.

Naturally, Paul's ministry was not without excitement and conflict. Many of the Jews reviled him and rejected his message. This was Paul's signal to denounce their unbelief and move on to minister to Gentiles. Though Paul's passion was for reaching the Gentiles with the gospel, he always first extended the message to the local synagogue wherever he went. Some of the Jews believed as well as many other Corinthians. It is implied that Paul shifted from preaching in the synagogues when he was rejected and began preaching to Corinthians in the market place. Their place of prayer and worship was in the home of Aquila and Priscilla. Perhaps their home was also the place for Paul to teach the couple theology and doctrine. Paul knew that he would not always be with them and needed to disciple them accordingly.

Radical Christianity
In Paul's scheme of things there was no such thing as nominal Christianity. His converts started churches, suffered persecution, and often followed him to the mission field. The spirit filled life meant empowerment for ministry, not just warm fuzzy feelings of belonging. This is important to understand before we see the kind of woman Priscilla was. She came to Christ through Paul's teaching. She and her husband opened their home not only to the Apostle, but to all the believers in their town. They ran a business and learned Christian doctrine from Paul. What was going on in Paul's mind? What might his hopes have been as he prayed and dreamed about future ministry plans? What part would his hosts play in the emergence of the church of Jesus Christ?

After much controversy in Paul's ministry in Corinth (cf. Acts 18:5-17) he leaves Corinth. In verse 18 we are told that Paul is accompanied by "Priscilla and Aquila." Much has been made by scholars of the name order given in Acts 18 and two other Scripture references which mention Priscilla first. Feminist theologians attach egalitarian meaning to this on what I call a flimsy assertion that the author wants to credit spiritual dominance to Priscilla, rather than her husband. Not only does this fly in the face of Paul's teachings throughout the New Testament concerning male headship, through careful inductive study of the four relevant passages I am convinced that there are other possibilities. These possibilities are refreshingly more applicable to today's Christian woman than the bizarre interpretations of some feminist evangelicals who jump to the conclusion that it was Priscilla who taught and led in ministry.

The Home Church
Let's imagine the setting of Paul and his believing contemporaries who are radically committed to carry the Gospel of Jesus to their known world. For almost three centuries, most early church believers would have to rely on the Word of God to come from the mouths of the first Apostles. Only the fortunate few would be

able to read or listen to a reading of the four gospels or one of the Apostle's epistles. By at least 70 A.D. the geographically spread out New Testament authors had finished writing the books and epistles that would become known as the New Testament. But their works were not collected into one canon until about 325 A.D. This meant that the church had to be protected from heresy by the pure teaching of the Apostles. These men trained successors, and were careful to also train pastors and shepherds. Based on Acts 18, I believe Paul was training Aquila to be a pastor. What better on the job theological training could a man ask for than to have the Apostle Paul living in his home! Certainly Priscilla was privy to much of Paul's teaching and reasoning.

So, if it is true that Aquila was a kind of lay pastor, what does that make Priscilla? Her husband owns a tent making business that supports them financially. But their lives really revolve around ministry. There is no mention of children for the couple, but that is not necessarily significant. They are a couple who constantly open their home for ministry. They host regular gatherings of believers. They live off of tent making, but in Acts 18:18 they demonstrate that they don't live for it. Aquila is a preacher of the gospel and Priscilla is a pastor's wife. Can you grasp the importance and impact of a woman who is willing to embrace a highly controversial house guest and open her home to a myriad of followers shortly after moving to a new country? Can you envision the generous and submissive spirit of a lady who gladly forsakes earthly comforts for eternal pleasures (Ps. 16:11) in Christ? Priscilla was just that lady and she endeared herself to Paul. Her support and eagerness would have made Aquila's ministry possible.

The Home Arena of Ministry for Women
In Acts 18:18 "Priscilla and Aquila" set sail with Paul for Ephesus. I don't doubt that Priscilla had an excellent theology and a knowledge of the Hebrew Scriptures. I don't doubt that there were times when she sat at the feet of Paul and absorbed wisdom and lessons from him. She was likely to have been quite well educated.

She and her husband were likely to have been fairly cultivated and successful. They were self employed, practiced hospitality freely; and managed to relocate and get settled in new communities simply. Whether or not they had children only impacts how much concentrated time Priscilla could have devoted to other pursuits.

Unlike women of today, Priscilla's life would have been largely limited to her home and her neighborhood. With patience and creativity the following pursuits are surprisingly compatible to the goal of being like the virtuous woman of Proverbs 31: exploring and researching issues; scholarly study; reading widely; entertaining and hospitality in the home; domestic work for the family in the home; tending to the needs of children and husband; sewing; pitching in with the family business; gardening; organizing and creating a loving home. Precisely because of her likely role of home based nurturer Priscilla would have been able to pursue many outlets of interests, with great freedom to prioritize according to the needs of her family. Women who have children and full time careers outside the home rarely have time for hobbies, neighbors, and in depth interests with out pilfering from the family's tranquility. As providence would have it, homemakers have more opportunity to freelance and explore their gifts and interests than women who are obligated to employers!

I don't see any reason for Priscilla to have to be the dominant one in her marriage in order to shine. Surely Aquila loved his wife and wanted her to use her gifts. Maybe this was in response to something he received from her. We wives and mothers need to be careful not to expect that our families should be thrilled about our pursuits when they become a hindrance to domestic harmony. It is part of our sacrificial call to put things on hold when there is a conflict with priorities. Serving the needs of a family may not always be special in the world's eyes, but it is the thing that wins a husband's heart. Think about it! Are you going out of your way to help or do things for your husband that you suspect he'd enjoy but is afraid to ask for? Do you take the time to thank him for little things he does for the family? Do you extend warmth and affection to him regardless of how you feel? I find it hard to see what a Christian woman can really offer in ministry of any kind if she is not giving of herself to her husband and children sacrificially and joyfully!

When Paul and his partners in ministry reached Ephesus Paul went straight to the synagogue and reasoned with the Jews. They wanted him to stay longer, but he declined saying, "I will return to you if God wills." Paul followed the leading of the Lord. One must assume his disciples Priscilla and Aquila did also. As if they had agreed to be the missionaries in his absence once he had laid the groundwork in his teaching in the synagogue, they remained and waited for God to bring in the harvest of souls.

God Must Convert the Evangelist!
Based on Acts 18:24 it seems that Aquila and his wife joined with the local synagogue where Paul taught when they had first arrived in Ephesus. Paul had impeccable credentials (Acts 23:3; 26:4-5) and would have been well received, at least initially. The Christ following Jews would meet with their fellow Jews at the synagogue and make contacts with the Jewish community. Imagine that the couple were waiting to see God answer their prayer for one soul to come to Christ. Picture their excitement in hearing of Apollos from Alexandria. When Apollos came to town I suspect all the Jewish community came out to see and hear the articulate and brilliant man.

In Acts 18:24 Apollos was eloquent and competent in the Scriptures. He was instructed in the way of the Lord. I think this means he was educated by the finest and godliest that Alexandria had to offer. Alexandria was the birthplace of the first public library. It was the home of the greatest university in the Greco Roman world. The Jewish community there was larger than that of Jerusalem. The Greek speaking Jews of Alexandria commissioned the translation of the Hebrew Torah into the Greek Septuagint. This was the city of Philo, a Jewish philosopher and contemporary of Paul's. The Jewish community in Alexandria, Egypt not only had many beautiful synagogues, they had their own beautiful temple! So naturally, Apollos was expected to be top notch. And he did not fail to entrance his listeners.

He was fervent in spirit, meaning he was passionate and flowed with energy. He spoke compellingly and "accurately concerning Jesus," though his knowledge ended with what he had learned from John the Baptist! I gather that his references to the coming Messiah were understood by Priscilla and her husband to be about Jesus!

When the message of "repent for the kingdom of God is at hand" flowed from Apollos' lips, Priscilla and Aquila must have nearly exploded with excitement. He must have been taught by someone who had heard John preach! Apollos must have studied the messianic prophecies in great detail! He must have been baptized for the repentance of sins in the tradition of John the Baptist! In Acts 18:26 Apollos "began to speak boldly in the synagogue, but when Priscilla and Aquila heard him, they took him and explained to him the ways of God more accurately."

With all the excitement surrounding his message concerning the kingdom of God, how exactly would they "take him and explain the ways of God more accurately"? I believe they would seek him out and welcome him to town. Priscilla would immediately invite Apollos over for dinner. She would make an incredible meal and give her husband an opportunity to unfold to Apollos the Gospel of Jesus Christ. Together they would explain to him the teaching they had received from Paul. Maybe he visited frequently. Maybe he even lived with them. Certainly he was introduced to other Jewish Christ followers in the home of Priscilla and Aquila. He embraced Jesus, sat under Aquila's teaching, and expressed to the "brothers" in Acts 18:27 a desire to preach in Achaia (Greece) across the Aegean Sea and was encouraged by them to do so. Apollos was very effective in leading people to saving faith. He "powerfully" refuted the Jews who did not accept Jesus in public debates. Thanks to the missionary couple in Ephesus Apollos was thoroughly trained in the gospel of Jesus the Christ.

The Emerging Gospel
The Holy Spirit was moving in much the same way in other regions. We are told in Acts 19 that Paul had a similar experience when he met up with twelve men in upper Ephesus who were like Apollos and had never heard the entire gospel of Jesus. They were "disciples" but Paul had to ask if they had received the Holy Spirit when they believed. This implies that in the Apostle's eyes they seemed to be lacking something. The men "had not even heard that there is a Holy Spirit"! Paul questioned further and learned that they were baptized into John's baptism. This explained a lot! So Paul unfolded to them the full gospel, explained that Jesus was the Messiah that John the Baptist preached about, and baptized them in the name of the Lord Jesus. According to verse 6, "When Paul had laid his hands on them, the Holy Spirit came on them, and they began speaking in tongues and prophesying. There were about twelve men in all." The Spirit of God came upon them powerfully to empower them for ministry. But before they could go out they must train under Paul.

For three months they watched Paul as he preached in the synagogue boldly, reasoning and persuading the Jews of this region about the kingdom of God. What a homiletics class that must have been! They also got to see how Paul dealt with those who would stubbornly refuse to believe. He withdrew from those who were exposed to the gospel and persisted in unbelief and took the disciples to a public meeting hall to present the gospel on a daily basis. These men listened to Paul for several hours a day with many local residents listening and spreading the word of Paul's preaching. This went on for two years! "All the residents of Asia heard the word of the Lord, both Jews and Greeks." God was building his church on the work of his Apostles.

A Greeting From Corinth and Rome
When Paul was in Corinth again he wrote to the church in Rome. The book of Romans is Paul's treatise on God's sovereign grace. In chapter 16 the Apostle takes the time to send word from some

of his closest co-laborers in Christ. In Romans 16:3-5 we learn a great deal about Paul's love and respect for those who have become brothers and sisters in Christ and his work. "Greet Prisca and Aquila, my fellow workers in Christ Jesus, who risked their necks for my life, to whom not only I give thanks but all the churches of the Gentiles give thanks as well. Greet also the church in their house." Paul's reference to the couple risking their necks for his life is a fascinating mystery. I don't think Paul was exaggerating. It seems that he and all the churches felt indebted to them for saving his life.

This was something very special from Paul toward a daughter, sister, and fellow servant in Christ. I think he loved both she and her husband, but it was Priscilla, or "little Prissy" that held a special place in his heart. Did she do his laundry when he lived in their home? Might the thoughtful hostess have made Paul his favorite foods, or guarded against too many interruptions while he prayed or slept? Many a pastor's wife has blazed the way for ministry with hospitality and bubbly personality! Certainly Prisca endeared herself to Paul with her adorable personality, brave commitment, and nurturing sacrifice.

From Rome, Paul gives another similar greeting to the same lady and her husband in 2 Timothy 4:19: "Greet Prisca and Aquila, and the household of Onesiphorus..." Could it be that "little Prissy" was known and loved not only by Paul, but all who came into contact with her and Aquila? Aquila is not at all diminished by Paul's and Luke's esteem for his splendid wife! It has always been proper and highly complimentary for a bachelor to give high praise to a friend's wife. I do think Paul somewhat singles out Priscilla, but not for the reasons we in our post modern culture might assume. Paul is partial to Priscilla not to indicate her dominance in leadership, but rather to esteem her worth as an extraordinary sister and servant in Christ—whatever her particular gifts may have been!

The Pastor's Wife

In 1 Corinthians 16:19 Paul sends official greetings from the churches of Asia: "The churches of Asia send you greetings. Aquila and Prisca, together with the church in their house, send you hearty greetings in the Lord. All the brothers and sisters send you greetings. Greet one another with a holy kiss." Certainly there were many house churches, but it is clear that the one in Aquila's house is led by Aquila. The ebullient wording of the greeting suggests a vibrant and loving congregation. Let us not forget the endearing and adorable pastor's wife, "Prisca." She has complemented her husband's ministry beautifully. She has responded to the call of the gospel eagerly. Priscilla has been a friend and sister to Apostles. She is a superb example of the drive for ministry placed in the heart of a godly woman.

The world of Pricilla was full of idolatry, corruption, and injustice. When she and Aquila became Christians, they would have gradually and sometimes instantly, been cut off from their own Jewish people. They opened their home to other believers in Jesus. They embraced not only Christ, but his Apostle Paul and his teaching. On this teaching they helped to build the Church of Jesus Christ.

The Command of Hospitality

After all of our reading and studying, we don't really know specifically what Priscilla's gifts, talents, and interests were. We can speculate and assume the best about her varied contributions to the kingdom, but I assume she was like us in her struggle to prioritize and find meaning in everyday tasks. We live in a society that does not highly value the humble and common work of tending children, cooking, pulling weeds, cleaning, and grocery shopping. People joke about how "somebody has to do it", but it is usually implied that the job could be done by anyone. Since hospitality was likely practiced a great deal by Priscilla, let's take a look at God's big picture concerning the role of hospitality.

In Romans 12:9-13 we have Paul's definition of Christian

hospitality: "Let love be genuine. Abhor what is evil; hold fast to what is good. Love one another with brotherly affection. Outdo one another in showing honor. Do not be slothful in zeal, be fervent in spirit, and serve the Lord. Rejoice in hope, be patient in tribulation, be constant in prayer. Contribute to the needs of the saints and seek to show hospitality." It is in homes or home like settings (even a restaurant or park) that Christians can move from being acquaintances to friends. It is not really an option in the church, it is a command. Paul doesn't present hospitality as a special gift to be practiced by the gifted. It is a command for us to be genuinely loving, generous, and hospitable. Have you ever noticed that before?

In Hebrews 12:1-3 Paul gives an even bigger picture for hospitality: "Let brotherly love continue. Do not neglect to show hospitality to strangers, for thereby some have entertained angels unawares. Remember those who are in prison, as though in prison with them, and those who are mistreated, since you also are in the body." Once again, hospitality is a command for the Church. We use it with each other, with strangers, in our homes, out in the world, and in the prisons and dreadful places where the love and beauty of Christ must be taken. When we cannot bring people in, we go to them.

In Scripture God seems to assume that hospitality isn't easy or convenient. He warns against burnout in 1 Peter 4:9: "Show hospitality to one another without grumbling." He goes on to say that everyone should use their gifts to serve one another. It seems that our gifts are to be exercised largely in the context of hospitality. And the gifts are varied ways of facilitating hospitality and the greater work of God's kingdom. The methods we may use are plentiful as long as we don't over impose on family members or neglect our duties.

The Today Priscillas
It is thrilling for women seeking to be busy at home (cf. Titus 2:5) to see that their contributions, whether noticed by others or

not, can be of vital importance to the kingdom of God. It is in the home that we women can uniquely shine for the glory of God. Here are some examples:

In the home we are free to bring people together and set a topic of dialogue at dinner. We can plan ahead so that the environment is pleasing and yet our attention is on our guests. Or sometimes the better strategy is to be very casual and spontaneous to put others at ease. We can be intentional about including neighbors when we have church fellowships. We can invite the mom of our child's friend to stay a while for tea when she comes to drop off or pick up her child for a play date. We can invite someone over for coffee when we meet a new woman at church; even better, invite a couple of moms with comparable aged children if she is new to the area. We can look for new faces at church or community events and introduce ourselves. Send notes to people to follow up conversations or let people know you are praying for them when you have heard they are having hard times. All of these things require intentional, proactive effort.

There is little excuse for feeling like one is wasting away in isolation at home. Some of that feeling is understandable and tolerable if kept in a healthy perspective. Do your children really mind or suffer if you aren't fulfilled? Is it really hurting you to focus on the needs of others? Keep alert for opportunities in which you can cultivate from home areas of interests. Use nap times to research topics for personal study and growth on the internet. We can save time and stress by shopping on the internet. We can email and network via computers. We can write and organize newsletters, essays, books, women's and children's studies, community events, and etc, etc, etc... If we use our resources responsibly the information age can open up worlds of opportunity for personal growth and ministry for stay at home moms and retirees. With a positive attitude and creativity we can optimize our time at home and tend the needs of family.

Facilitators

Not everyone is able to or interested in inviting people to their home. We can facilitate ministry by helping out when someone invites us to their home. We can knock ourselves out once in a while and take something really special and generous, instead of the bare minimum, to a meeting or pot luck! Nothing is more appreciated to a hostess than a helper who intuitively knows what needs to be done without having to be told! There are lots of practical ways to be gracious in hospitality without having to host gatherings in one's home.

Fueling the Drive

We who are stay at home moms or retirees are privileged to have more options in making time for Scripture study and prayer. Whenever your kids interrupt you, start reading to them and sharing what you are studying. Sweetly invite them to join you in prayer if they don't respect your time with God. They will either be enriched by your devotional and study activities directly, or they will be enriched in knowing that their mom is serious about knowing God and that they better be respectful! Mothering, wifely love, and serving in the home give opportunity for many spiritual insights. There is nothing boring or menial about being a loving wife and mother if you are a daughter of God. Even if you only have a few minutes to hold a Bible in your hands, meditation and prayer can take place while washing dishes, planting flowers, and holding a child. As his child you are aware that he sees our hearts, knows our motives, and rewards us for our good deeds, as Hebrews 4:13 so aptly tells us.

If you are not compelled to spend time in God's word and pray for your family and others, then you are not driven by God to do anything! Of course, one has to be doing something challenging to need God! Are you stepping out in faith to obey God daily? Are you in need of strength to meet your husband's needs? Are you feeling challenged because of a commitment to excellence? If you are just living to please yourself then you might not need prayer and direction. But the woman who is trusting God with difficult things in her life is dependant on God's word. She crave it, loves it, longs for it, yearns for it, desires it, plans for it, lives for it, obeys it! There is no imperative about how long, how frequently, or how noticeable our time in Scripture must be, just as there is no rule that one must eat at every opportunity! Ouch! I think a Priscilla is motivated by a hunger and thirst for God. Like David in Psalm 42:2 she "pants for God and cries to Him and pours out her soul to Him and sings songs of praise to him." She doesn't wallow in depression forever! She talks to herself and says, "Hope in God; for I shall again praise Him." (Ps. 42:5)

A Priscilla must extend herself to others. She is not self focused, but God focused. She is a vessel of God's grace and love. She cannot be this to her family and others if she is not saturated with God's word. When the well is running dry she knows where to fetch from the living water of Jesus in prayer. She knows her Bible enough to find key passages and take delight in the law of the Lord. God is her refuge. She is only as good as her time with God is consistent. In pursuing God, we tap into the surest form of spiritual and emotional health. We need to encourage each other in the spiritual disciplines.

Ask the Name

In the New Testament the church was usually held in homes. I think the use of homes and public spaces for church gatherings was providential. God knew that people would be intrigued by anything happening in the public square and that home is the place to knit hearts further together in study, prayer, and fellowship. Though we in the church are now able to hold meetings in large buildings that are corporately owned, it would be appropriate to see our local church as an extension of our own homes. After all, the church is our spiritual family, so we might work like mini hostesses at church and extend ourselves to others, especially visitors and new folks.

Make a point of remembering names. This is hard for everyone so don't let "I'm so bad at names" be your excuse. The reality is one has to want to know the names of others. In John 10:3 Jesus promises to call his own sheep by name. Jesus would often call a person by name to compel them to listen. If our names are important to God, then we should make it a priority too. So admit it when your memory needs to be refreshed and just ask again. That usually gives the other person a sense of relief! It is also a polite indication that you want to know and be reminded—which is better than behaving as if it doesn't matter! A socially aloof attitude should be unheard of in the Body of Christ. Use people's names when you see them. Rack your brain, pressure yourself some, discreetly ask a friend if they remember the name; and do whatever it takes to be personable as a hostess in the kingdom of God! This is an important aspect of ministry that is often forgotten.

And then take it to the next level of social discourse by introducing people to each other. Include people in conversations. Call people by name whether from afar or up close. The more you call someone by name, the more others around you hear and remember the name. Refer to your husband by name instead of "him"! In fact, pronouns like "he" or "she" are not that polite except after the person's name has been clearly used. Fill in a newcomer on the brief details of a group conversation. Help people feel that they are wanted and valued. Nothing is more insulting than to be treated with indifference! Ask people about themselves and talk to them about what interests them. Just because you may be meeting someone in a church building doesn't mean that the topic of conversation has to be church related. It requires stepping out of one's comfort zone to relate to people on their level.

If you lead a woman's Bible study call people to let them know they have been missed. Their absence may be a subconscious test on their part to see if Christians really care! Call people by name in a group setting to help others remember names. Use name tags but don't rely on name tags—they are a crutch. Don't be passive and just hope you don't have to use a name! Rely on conversation, memory triggers, reminders from discreet friends, pictorial directories, and humility in asking one more time! Some people think etiquette and names are a minor point. That is true for rude people. I bet if we women took the lead in making names a priority our men would appreciate it. Our pastor's wives are probably already doing it for their husbands! Until recent history, it has always been the domain of women to be the arbiters of manners and tradition.

More Than a Cup of Coffee
In our society in which everyone senses that they have to fend for themselves and be self sufficient, we need a vision for "seeking to show hospitality" akin to Paul's command in Romans 12. When women are invited to attractively displayed tables of delicious treats that someone volunteered to prepare—this is serving a woman's need to experience beauty. When we smile and embrace a woman as she comes into the room for an event or fellowship—we are ministering to her womanly longing for sisters in Christ. When we lovingly and firmly teach to each other God's word—we are meeting the need every woman has for truth. These acts and others like them are not mere tasks that need to be performed dutifully—they are practical and powerful ways to bring glory to God! Women minister to each other graciously by doing things that soften our hearts to God and each other.

Through friendly initiative and hospitality Christian women hold the key to reaching out to women who might be depressed, lonely, and bored. Frankly, who hasn't felt those things! We need to step out of our isolation and self absorption and get together with other women. This is where Christian women can really demonstrate Christ's love by being a friend to someone spontaneously.

A Truly Big Love!
Christian hospitality seeks creative ways to practice or facilitate making people feel included, important, loved, and valued in God's eyes. Hospitality is much bigger than setting something

up and attending. It is more than organization and planning. It is more than entertaining. Hospitality is about acting out the love of Christ. It is a joyful and often sacrificial way of nurturing life. Whether it's in your own home, some else's, or in a church building, we women have a privilege and responsibility to lead the way in nurturing our families and others by ministering in this way. May the Spirit of God lead a movement of womanly nurture in our churches and communities! May this be our drive for ministry!

Think of the many hidden talents you may discover about yourself if you were to make biblical hospitality a priority. Imagine the deeper conversations and friendships that will develop as a result of extending yourself and home to others. It may start with a note. It may involve a little time invested on the phone. It may encourage better housekeeping. It may lead to a cup of tea. It may blossom into authentic relationships. It may lead to a Bible study or prayer group. It may lead to revival!

Paul's Love for Priscilla
Is it too simplistic to assume that Paul's love for Priscilla might have had greatly to do with her hospitality and wifely devotion to Aquila? Is it not possible that her foremost contribution to the kingdom was in supporting her pastor husband and welcoming others into their home? This may have been in addition to other offerings as well. But why do many believe that Priscilla's contributions are puzzling or non traditional? I think it is because women, over the past century, have bought into the lie that only high salaried, credentialed, and authoritative roles are vital. In our search for importance we have become less effective as women; less feminine; less giving—and less Priscilla, the very woman many claim as their model!

May our homes be a haven for ministry and an exciting arena in which we develop gifts as women that will be a complement to our families and the work of God's kingdom. May we truly value and encourage the generous and loving women in the body of Christ who nurture others in ministry. May we be fueled by a Bible saturated desire to know God deeply and serve him joyfully. May we women return to the uniquely feminine drive for ministry found among Jesus' women followers in the New Testament.

Questions for Study and Discussion:

1. Please turn to Acts 17:16-34. When Paul was in Athens he was waiting for his fellow missionaries to meet him and then depart together for Corinth. In 17:16-17 what two things does Paul do in response to the Athenian culture? Explain how Paul's mode of operation is an example for believers.

2. Acts 18:1-3 is our introduction to Aquila and Priscilla. Paul must have been overjoyed to witness to and serve with Aquila and his wife. How might ministry and fellowship between believers be affected if it were automatic for us to put ourselves on the line the way Paul and other early church believers did?

3. Please turn to Acts 18:9-11. What (or who) was the assurance given to Paul?

4. In Acts 18:21 Paul defers to _____ _____. Does it strike you as amazing that the great Apostle Paul did not know everything about God's will?! How are his words and actions an encouragement and example for us?

5. In Acts 18:24-28, we have a description of the church in Ephesus under the leadership of Aquila. In regards to Apollo's ministry how did they contribute?

6. Please read Romans 16 in which Paul greets and makes reference to the many people he has led in ministry. Beginning with Phoebe and ending with verse 23 list any specific remarks Paul makes about each person.

7. What kind of leader would you say Paul was?

8. Based on Romans 16:3-5 what qualities did the church started by Aquila and Priscilla possess?

9. 1 Corinthians 16:19-20 is an official greeting from Paul on

behalf of Aquila the pastor, his wife, and the church that meets in their house.

What does the inclusion of "Prisca" suggest to you about Paul's style of ministry and value for the pastor's wife?

What are some hints from these verses to explain Paul's love for this pastor and his church?

10. 1 Timothy 2:8-15 is Paul's principle of masculine leadership in the church. How does this play out for women who might be gifted in leadership? Please support your answer with examples or verses from Scripture.

11. In terms of positives, what is I Timothy telling women they can and should do?

12. Read Romans 12:9-13. List some ways that women, whether single or married, can fulfill these verses in or from the home.

13. John 10:3 says that Jesus knows the name of his sheep.

    How does it make you feel to have someone (besides a telemarketer) remember your name?

    What is the relationship between the name and intimacy?

    On whose name shall we call if we are able? (Isaiah 41:25-26)

    What happens to those who don't know and confess The Name?! (Acts 4:12)

14. In Titus 2:3-5 we women are given an outline for women's ministry. List the things that older women are to teach the younger women.

15. Paul tells the older women to lead in this regard. Is this role of leadership still open and needed to women?

16. Why should women show hospitality to each other? What is its effect?

17. Considering that Priscilla was revered and spoken of along with her husband frequently, what kind of leader do you imagine Aquila to have been?

18. 1 Peter 3:7 is the verse in which the phrase has been coined "the weaker vessel." As a woman do you take personal offense at this description? Explain.

19. What does it mean to be a daughter of Sarah?

12

RAHAB: SAVED ALIVE BY THE WONDERS OF GOD

Scripture References:
Numbers 13-14 • Joshua 1-6

The God of the Bible is known for press releases and publicity stunts. He performs mighty wonders in order to draw attention to Himself. In His case, the attention is justified. He is the holiest, and most glorious Being in the entire universe. He is the great "I Am" as told to Moses in Exodus 3:14. Through Moses God performed miraculous deeds to bring his people out of bondage in Egypt. Ten devastating plagues, the mass exodus, and the parting of the Red Sea all served to demonstrate God's power to his people and a watching world. Manna from heaven, water from rocks, and the Ten Commandments served as God's merciful provision and direction for His chosen people. Through Moses he showed them that they would go back to the land he had promised their fathers Abraham, Isaac, and Jacob. They would return to that Promised Land and God would give it to them—and along the way they would make the nations around them very aware of God's glory.

In Numbers 13 the Lord tells Moses to send men to spy out the land of Canaan. So Moses sent out heads of each tribe to learn the condition of the land and the strength of the people of Canaan. They went during the season of the first ripe grapes. When the spies returned after forty days they reported that the land "flows with milk and honey." However, they said, the people of the land are strong; their cities are fortified and very large. We even saw giants there, they reported. And to top off everything else, some of their cities (like Jericho) have the strategic advantage of dwelling along the Jordan River! How would they ever get across the Jordan?

To the majority of these spies the promises of God were not enough to conquer the intimidating Canaanites and their equally fierce neighbors. In the assembly of the congregation people raised a loud cry and wept. The people of Israel grumbled against Moses and Aaron. How dare their leaders get them into this mess! They and their families left Egypt only to die. The frightened people demanded another leader so that they could high tail it back to Egypt, of all places! Moses and Aaron fell on their faces before all the people.

But fortunately, there was dissent among the spies. There were two brave men who had also been to Canaan and brought back an entirely different perspective. With passion and daring, Joshua and Caleb tore their clothes before all assembled and declared, "'The land, which we passed through to spy it out, is an exceedingly good land. If the Lord delights in us, he will bring us into this land and give it to us, a land that flows with milk and honey. Only do not rebel against the Lord. And do not fear the people of the land, for they are bread for us. Their protection is removed from them, and the Lord is with us; do not fear them.' Then all the congregation said to stone them with stones. But the glory of the Lord appeared at the tent of meeting to all the people of Israel." God punished his people for their lack of faith by promising that "none of those who have seen my glory and my signs that I did in Egypt and in the wilderness, and yet have put me to the test these ten times shall see the land that I swore to give to their fathers." In fact all the spies who grumbled against the Lord died by plague before the Lord. Only Joshua and Caleb remained alive.

When some of the people regretted their lack of faith, and went up to the hill country of Canaan to engage in battle, they further incurred the wrath of God. The Lord would not go with them and they lost in battle to the Amalekites and the Canaanites. The Promised Land would only come to them on God's terms!

The Promise Fulfilled
Forty years later Joshua becomes Moses' successor. In Joshua 1:10 Joshua commands the people to prepare provisions for in three days they would "pass over this Jordan to go in to take possession of the land that the Lord your God is giving you to possess." We are told in the English Standard Version translation that Joshua "had sent" two men secretly to spy out the land, especially Jericho. It seems that Joshua might have decided, based on his own experiences, to keep this spy mission a secret to prevent the Israelites from being disheartened in the event of a bad report from the spies. Bad report or not, everything depended on God's power and timing!

Rahab : The Prostitute
Rahab is referred to in the New Testament three times. Her name is listed in Matthew 1:5 in the genealogy of Christ. In Hebrews 11:30-31 and James 2:25 Rahab is described as a prostitute. In Joshua 2:1 Rahab is clearly depicted as a prostitute. That is not to say that is all she was. She owned a house, probably a lodging house, or inn. Until the twentieth century, an inn or boarding house might include the shady trade of prostitution, though not all patrons would participate in that feature. Hence the name, "house of ill repute." Consequently, moral business owners would make a major point of advertising their establishments as places of good reputation. Scripture is very clear on the nature of Rahab's sinful background.

I would also speculate that Rahab's prostitution is not the stereotypical prostitution seen in western civilization. She owns her own house, or inn. Thus we might gather that she is, or was at one time, financially well off. The location of her home, built into the city wall, suggests privilege or advantageous location. Also, she deeply cares for her family. This all leads to one possibility that I think is worth considering: perhaps Rahab's father is unable to provide for his family and Rahab has opened their house to lodgers and taken up prostitution to bring in money. Women in her day had few means to support themselves. Conversely, since male and female prostitution was a central part of Canaanite religion and society, Rahab's occupation may not have been taboo in their culture.

In Joshua 2:6, there is the interesting reference to stalks of flax drying on the roof of the inn. This may have been part of a cottage industry in which the women of the family pressed the seeds of the flax plant into oil and spun the fiber into thread. The thread could be dyed and made into cords, tassels, and linen. This honest, upright occupation with fine crafts would be used to glorify God.

Rahab's house was strategically located in the wall of Jericho. Built right into the city's fortifications was the house itself with windows facing outward. When the King of Jericho heard that spies were seen going into Rahab's house he sent a messenger ordering her to put the men out. He thought he could count on this prostitute to follow orders. He thought she would want to stay out of danger and keep the status quo. After all, hers is a business that thrives on malevolence and sleaze—vices prized by their very pagan society. But the king doesn't get to Rahab first. Somehow, it is the spies who have already won her loyalty in a brief encounter.

Rahab's apparent gift of making lodgers comfortable was used by God. She would be aware of their needs and serve them with food and hospitality. She would hide the spies and deceive the evil pursuers to save them. She would talk to them and ascertain their plans and intentions. These womanly gifts of hospitality, not prostitution, would be used to glorify God.

Could it be that when the spies came into her house sincerely wanting a place to lodge and learn the local news Rahab would have been intrigued by men who were not interested in anything else? Could she tell by their appearance and behavior that they were different? As godly and brave Jewish men, their treatment of Rahab would have been different from what she received from her usual patrons. Whatever transpired between them, when the king's men arrived, Rahab had already decided where her loyalties lay. The men were safely hidden away on her roof under her drying stalks of flax. In order to save the Israelite spies, Rahab lies and tricks the men into leaving the city to pursue the spies. The focus of this account is not the lie, but the intent behind it. This is one lie that would go down in history as an act of faith and obedience to God.

Rahab's Confession
In Joshua 2:8 Rahab goes up to the roof to speak to the men she's hiding. Here they are trapped in her home and not exactly free to scout out the city. But they can see a lot from her roof–and they will learn plenty about her country and her people right where they are.

Rahab, the prostitute says to the men, "'I know that the Lord has given you the land, and that the fear of you has fallen upon us, and that all the inhabitants of the land melt away before you. For we have heard how the Lord dried up the water of the Red Sea before you when you came out of Egypt, and what you did to the two kings of the Amorites who were beyond the Jordan, to Sihon and Og, whom you devoted to destruction. And as soon as we heard it, our hearts melted, and there was no spirit left in any man because of you, for the Lord your God, He is God in the heavens above and on the earth beneath. Now then, please swear to me by the Lord that, as I have dealt kindly with you, you also will deal kindly with my father's house, and give me a sure sign that you will save alive my father and mother, my brothers and sisters, and all who belong to them, and deliver our lives from death.' And the men said to her, 'Our life for yours even to death! If you do not tell this business of ours, then when the Lord gives us the land we will deal kindly and faithfully with you.'"

All of this between a pagan prostitute and two godly men—it boggles the mind!

I believe God had been working on Rahab's heart for a long time. Perhaps she was tired of the lies and corruption of her own life. Certainly there would be no hope of changing or improving her predicament within the walls of her own home or city. Like her fellow citizens, Rahab has heard the many legends and rumors about the Israelites and their escape from Egypt. She has heard about the power, righteousness, and zero tolerance of the Lord. She is motivated by fear. When those men came into her establishment, God compelled her to open up to them and vice versa. She knows that the Israelite's power is in their God. If only God's people could have seen that themselves years before! Could this have been what the Lord wanted the spies to discover? That a sinful enemy woman was ready to defect to their side and turn to them for protection? That her people were reportedly resigned to defeat? That they could count on instant victory because the people of Jericho were starting to figure out what Joshua had told his own people in Numbers 14:9: "their protection is removed from them, and the Lord is with us; do not fear them". You know God is on the move when many who don't know him are shaking for fear of him.

I surmise this must have had a powerful and affirming effect on the spies. They exchanged vows of loyalty with Rahab. They promised that her entire family, those inside her house, would be saved during the invasion. But she would have to leave a sign. It was agreed that the sign would be a scarlet cord, perhaps made of flax, in the window. This would be the sign of their vow and of her faith in their God.

Rahab's Oath

Rahab's home was strategically located in the wall of Jericho. The wall was the chief fear of the Israelites. They saw the wall as insurmountable. Earlier, Rahab had warned (2:16) the spies that they should "go into the hills, or the pursuers will encounter you, and hide there three days until the pursuers have returned." Before letting the men down by a rope through a window, the men spell out the conditions of the vow they have made with Rahab.

In Joshua 2:17-21, the men outlined the following: 1) When we come into the land tie this scarlet cord in the window through which you let us down. 2) Gather into your house every member of your father's household. 3) If anyone goes out into the street his blood shall be on his own head, not ours. 4) If a hand is laid on anyone in this house his blood shall be on our head. 5) But if you tell this business of ours, we will not be held responsible to this oath. Rahab responded with, "According to your words, so be it." She sent them away and took the oath very seriously by tying the scarlet cord in the window. I wonder if Rahab felt respected by these men; if she sensed that they took her seriously.

So now Rahab has done something irrevocable. She has betrayed her king, country, and neighbors. Because of the work of God in her heart and conscience she has reached the point of spiritual realization in which one understands that God must come first. When God transforms one's way of thinking, paradigm shifts force us to see everything in a new light. But that new thinking must be accompanied by some sort of action or fruit. As taught by James in the New Testament, faith and works go hand in hand. This was clearly seen in the case of Rahab as James 2:24-25 points out: "You see that a person is justified by works and not by faith alone. And in the same way was not also Rahab the prostitute justified by works when she received the messengers and sent them out by another way?" Rahab, who had but a little knowledge to go on, expressed her faith when she testified to the spies about the God of Israel. When she helped them and tricked the authorities of her city, she was demonstrating her faith! What the Canaanites meant for their own protection, the Wall of Jericho, was in truth bondage for them. Walls may keep out enemies, but they also give those within a false sense of security.

Rahab's Advice

According to Joshua 2:22-24 the spies took Rahab's advice seriously. They went into the hills and returned three days later as she advised. The pursuers searched all along the way and found nothing. The spies came to Joshua the son of Nun and they told him all that had happened to them. Their message was, "Truly the Lord has given all the land into our hands. And also, all the inhabitants of the land melt away because of us." Beyond doubt, God's undercover agents had been impacted by Rahab's appraisal of things!

The Four Events

In reading closely the accounts of Joshua 1 through 6 the command from Joshua in chapter 1, verse 11, to prepare to cross the Jordan was precipitated by the return of the spies he had sent into Jericho. So it seems the positive report they gave to Joshua was just the news he needed.

In an effort to not leave out important background details, and yet not become bogged down, here is a summary of the four events (in bold) which lead up to the fall of Jericho.

As commanded by God, Joshua and all his people camped at the edge of the Jordan for three days. In Joshua 3:5 the leader announces, "Consecrate yourselves, for tomorrow the Lord will do wonders among you." They then had a very orderly and symbolic crossing of the Jordan River, with the people following the priests who carried the Ark of the Covenant. This is basically a reenactment of the crossing of the Red Sea by the Israelites when they were led by Moses. I wonder if the surrounding countries and neighbors ever scoffed at the Hebrews for failing to possess their "promised land"? I wonder if their wandering and continued sojourning of the outskirts was a point of ridicule from the pagan inhabitants. After all, the ten plagues, exodus from Egypt, parting of the Red Sea, and the miracles of God were great stories to listen to, even from the stand point of unbelievers. But what about some results! Wasn't this supposed to be about the so called people of God crossing the Red Sea to take possession of their so called promised land? Of course, the Israelites knew what the problem was. They had stubbornly and repeatedly disobeyed God along the way. Now, by crossing the Jordan, they would experience what their deceased relatives experienced when leaving Egypt. By crossing the Jordan they would have a chance to reverse the tide of faithlessness. They would send a warning to their watching world that their mighty God is on the move. His wonders are just beginning!

The second event was the setting up of a memorial in Gilgal, about one an a quarter miles from Jericho. They set up a memorial of twelve stones taken from the Jordan River. Joshua gives this explanation, my paraphrase, to the people in Joshua 4:21-24, "… Tell your children that Israel passed over the Jordan and the Red Sea on dry ground to show the world that the Hand of the Lord is mighty and that you will fear the Lord your God forever…"

In fact, according to 5:1, as soon as the kings of this region heard that the Lord had dried up their prime defense against the Israelites, their "hearts melted and there was no longer any spirit in them because of the people of Israel." No more scoffing from them!

The third event was the circumcision of all the males who were born on the way in the wilderness after they had come out of Egypt. It was the grandchildren of the first exodus that God saved to whom he would give the land. This should have been a bad sign to the generation in between—God didn't even tell Moses to bother circumcising them! Now Joshua must oversee the procedure and follow the law to the letter on all the nation. After three days of recovering in the camp, God told Joshua in 5:9, "Today I have rolled away the reproach of Egypt from you." Yes, I think the Hebrew people had become used to the ridicule of their neighbors for failing in their original mission. When we follow up our salvation by taking care of the business of spiritual growth and discipline, we fulfill the purpose of the grace of God in our lives. The Israelites had a cloud of shame over them for not fulfilling the original mission of leaving Egypt to return to the Promised Land. God's mission for us is to become his children by grace and begin to do the work of growing in faith and obedience.

The fourth event is the keeping of the Passover. Now the Hebrews can worship God in a bold and fresh way. They can remember their history and renew their faith. God gives the people a sign that probably gave them vigor and confidence for what was ahead: In verse 1 the manna from heaven ceases on the day after Passover. They begin to eat the produce of the land. Think about it—they are in the land they are about to fight for. They are not hiding. They are not fearful of living off the land. They are eating of its rich produce—they are amassing strength less than a mile and a half from Jericho! Each of these events was a vastly successful press release for the Lord.

The Commander of the Lord's Army

In Joshua 5:13-16, an extraordinary thing happens to Joshua. With retreat impossible now that they have crossed the Jordan, his fighting men waiting for further orders; and intense preoccupation with the coming battle, Joshua stands by Jericho and sees a man standing before him with his drawn sword in his hand. Joshua approached the man and said, "Are you for us, or for our adversaries?" And the man said, "No; but I am the commander of the army of the Lord. Now I have come." And Joshua fell on his face to the ground and worshipped him. Theologians believe this is a "Christophony," or preincarnate appearance of Jesus. The being would not have permitted Joshua to worship him if it were a mere angel. The words of the commander have a familiar ring to those spoken to Moses as he was astounded by a burning bush, "Take off your sandals from your feet, for the place where you are standing is holy." Of course, Joshua did so! God was empowering Joshua with a preview of His glory. He was assuring him that He was with him just as He was with Moses.

The Fall of Jericho

Consequently, Jericho was under siege. A self imposed cordon out of fear of the very people they used to mock. The Lord tells Joshua in 6:2, "See, I have given Jericho into your hand, with its king and mighty men of valor." In the next few verses God lays out for Joshua the surprisingly simple instructions for conquering Jericho: "You shall march around the city, all the men of war going around the city once. Thus shall you do for six days. On the seventh day you shall march around the city seven times and then the priests shall blow the trumpets, then all the people shall shout with a great shout, and the wall of the city will fall down flat and the people shall go up and straight into the city." So everyday the armed men would wake up early, go to the city of Jericho, and silently march around its wall once. Then they would return to their camp for the night. This went on through the seventh day when they marched around the city seven times. Can you imagine the bewilderment of the city's citizens? Perhaps the Israelites are a bit mystified as well!

When the seventh trip around the city is completed Joshua says to the people in 6:16-18, "Shout, for the Lord has given you the city. And the city and all that is within it shall be devoted to the Lord for destruction. Only Rahab the prostitute and all who are with her in her house shall live, because she hid the messengers whom we sent." And they would know her house, in the midst of the rubble of a former wall, by the scarlet cord she had tied in the window. There was something good from Rahab's former life that would be used as a symbol of God's glory.

I believe that Rahab's name had spread among the Hebrew people. Her name was a beacon of hope to the underdogs who would come to defeat her people. They were given strict instructions to destroy every person and devote all the livestock and possessions to destruction. But not Rahab and her family—not the woman who had faith in their God!

In verses 22-25 Joshua sends the two men who had spied out the land to "Go into the prostitute's house and bring out from there the woman and all who belong to her, as you swore to her." So they brought out Rahab and her father and mother and brothers and all who belonged to her. They were taken out of the city and put outside the camp of Israel. The city and everything in it was burned with fire and everything in it. But Rahab the prostitute and her father's household and all who belonged to her, Joshua saved alive. According to Joshua 6:25, "She has lived in Israel to this day, because she hid the messengers whom Joshua sent to spy out Jericho."

Always the Prostitute?
It is curious that Scripture repeatedly refers to Rahab as the prostitute. She came to saving faith. She demonstrated that faith with good works. She was saved alive by Joshua. She lived in Israel and was incorporated into the line of David (Matt. 1:5). But she is always called a prostitute. This begs the question, "Why?" What is God's perspective on this?

I believe the answer is in Hebrews 11:29-30, "By faith the people crossed the Red Sea as if on dry land, but the Egyptians, when they attempted to do the same, were drowned. By faith the walls of Jericho fell down after they had been encircled for seven days. By faith Rahab the prostitute did not perish with those who were disobedient, because she had given a friendly welcome to the spies."

Each verse alludes to a person, or thing that does the opposite of what one would normally expect, respectively: the people of Israel, the Egyptians, the walls of Jericho, and Rahab the prostitute.

The rag tag, enslaved, and persecuted people of Israel actually crossed the Red Sea with no hindrance, while the mighty army of Egypt drowned in the same waters! How? By faith in the Lord.

The thirty foot high, insurmountable, and impenetrable walls surrounding Jericho and its mighty men of valor collapsed when the army of God simply marched around the city seven times! How? By faith in the Lord.

When God's spies went into enemy territory and were seen and pursued by the local authorities, they escaped with the help of an errant and pagan prostitute! How? By faith in the Lord.

If God saved Rahab from her sin when she put her repentance and trust in him, then why would he want to bring up her prostitution throughout Scripture? I believe it is because he wants to receive the glory for saving her. He doesn't want anyone to become forgetful of the odds against his nation of Israel. He doesn't want us to become distanced from the depravity of a woman who could not have possibly come to faith apart from the revelation of God. Perhaps otherwise we wouldn't appreciate the greatness of Rahab's faith and works.

Wall Crumbling Faith
And where does such faith come from? Why do some people have it? Largely because of the work of God to reveal himself to these people. Their faith was in response to Him. Their deeds were in response to his deeds. Their faith was in response to his promises. Why do we need the inspiration that comes from their faith? Because our God expects the same faith from us. He is still orchestrating his global plan and wants us to trust that we are a part of it too. In the least, the wall crumbling faith we want requires that we understand that the plan is not about us. It includes us if we will humbly join in God's race which will lead us to heaven with Jesus. I highly recommend reading aloud the Hebrews 11 chapter for a flash of God's glory in the lives of his faithful. It is hard to stay spiritually dry "surrounded by so great a cloud of witnesses."

God Still Uses Rahabs
When the people of God were preparing to cross the Jordan, Joshua declared, "Consecrate yourselves, for tomorrow the Lord will do wonders among you." There is nothing very special about living a life of selfishness or chasing after earthly pleasures. That is how most people live. And most people don't ever witness the glory of God. Most settle for the mediocrity of this life. Think of all the fearful, fickle, and faithless people who would not enter the Promised Land with Moses. They were the children of those who left Egypt. They should have known what God could do, but they couldn't rise above their fear. They missed out on "the Wonders".

Are you a woman who has been living outside of God's moral will? Have you sensed guilt and a yearning for forgiveness and a spiritual family? There is no sin God won't forgive when one is truly repentant. Like Rahab, learn the promises of God in Scripture. Ask God to forgive you because of the suffering of Jesus on the cross on your behalf. Understand that God longs to forgive and save sinners. He won't take away the consequences of bad choices or deeds, but he offers salvation and gives us a new life in Christ; a relationship with God that will give greater happiness and purpose than any earthly pleasure!

Godly Fear
Earlier it was pointed out that Rahab was very motivated by fear when she helped the spies. Yet her fear was poles apart from the fear of the Israelites when they feared the Canaanites and rebelled against Moses. Like all of her countrymen Rahab must have heard reports of the Israelites crossing the Red Sea and the Jordan. By God's grace her panic of the reports moved from mere fear to godly fear. God's love is better appreciated in the context of his holiness. Then we realize how merciful and gracious He is to us sinners!

God uses fear of his punishment to bring people to repentance. In our own country's history, we have sadly lost sight of God as one who has the right to exact punishment or judge sinners. Even religious people are tolerant of sin and eager to seem non critical of sinners. We Christians in post modern America are easily led away from the biblical vision of a holy God who won't tolerate sin. We should watch our language when we speak of our faith and Lord in public. Isn't it more comfortable to present God to others as if He were most interested in being liked or putting people at ease? That is not the God of Scripture.

The faith of Rahab was largely triggered by fear. Fear for herself and her family. It is fear that leads sinners to saving faith. God must have made known to her, her need for a savior. She must have taken some measure of hope in hearing that the mighty and jealous Lord of the Israelites was faithful to his own. Maybe he would save her too. Maybe she could join his family and make a fresh start.

Saved Alive

Hence, Joshua saved alive Rahab and her father's household. She became one of God's chosen people. Chosen to be an example of what God can do with a repentant sinner. God made Rahab holy, set her apart from the sin of her past, and saved her alive for his glory. According to Matthew 1:5, Rahab had a child by Salmon named Boaz. Boaz married Ruth and had a son named Obed. Obed became the father of Jesse, and Jesse the father of David the great king of Israel. This genealogical line continued to the birth of Jesus.

God is pleased and glorified to have a former prostitute in the line of David. God delights in bringing outsiders, orphans, and lost sheep into his family. And remember, all those who don't have a personal relationship with Jesus are lost, regardless of moral decency. Our pride in being good is despicable to God compared to the repentance of a guilty sinner. If you are smugly satisfied with your own good up bringing and reputation, pride is the foundation of all sin. May the call of repentance be heard by many Rahabs to come!

Questions for Study and Discussion:

Scripture references:
Joshua 1-6
Matthew 1:5—line of David
Hebrews 11:30-31—Rahab saved by her faith
James 2:25—Rahab saved by her works

1. Read Hebrews 11:30-31. Why were the people of God successful at crossing the Red Sea?

2. Read Joshua 1:16-17 to summarize the attitude of the people of God and contrast it with the earlier attitudes displayed when the people rebelled against Moses.

3. In the Hebrews passage what specific deed is credited to Rahab?

4. In James 2:25 what specific deed is credited to Rahab?

5. In any passage referenced is there criticism of Rahab? If so, explain.

6. What is the implied motivation of Rahab's behavior?

7. What is Rahab's main concern when she asks the spies for a favor in Joshua 2:11-13?

8. Based on Joshua how did the spies treat Rahab?

9. In Joshua 3:7 the Lord tells Joshua of his plan to exalt him. Why would this be important for Joshua and Israel?

10. What is meant by Joshua's words in 3:5, "Consecrate yourselves, for tomorrow the Lord will do wonders among you"?

11. How can Joshua 5:9 be applied to God's people today? Can you give a personal example?

12. The following verses talk about fear:

    Joshua 2:24 ; Joshua 6:1

    How would you characterize the fear in these passages?

    Is the fear leading to reverence of God?

13. Contrast the fear of the Canaanites with the "fear" in the following verses: Psalm 2:11; Proverbs 19:23 ; Psalm 111:10; Joshua 4:24

14. Based on 2 Corinthians 7:1 ; Philippians 2:12 ; what made Rahab's fear different from that of her countrymen's?

15. How do we reconcile godly fear with 1 John 3:15-21?

    In Philippians 3:8-11 Paul talks about the worthlessness of human righteousness compared to the righteousness of Christ. Ephesians 2:1-8 teaches that grace has made us alive through faith in Jesus. How does grace bring glory to God?

16. Please turn to Matthew 1:1-6a.

    Who was the son of Rahab?

    Who were the wife and son of Boaz?

    Who was Obed's grandson?

    What is the significance of this genealogy?

About the Author

Barbara B. Gardner is a devoted homemaker whose devotional writings, "Whispers of Grace," first appeared on her church's website. They grew and developed into the book you now are holding. She has been blessed with a loving husband, Todd, and four children: Justine, Joshua, Abigail and Annabelle, who range in age from twelve to nineteen. She lives in St. Joseph, Michigan.